GRIT FACTOR

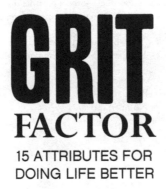

GRIT
FACTOR
15 ATTRIBUTES FOR DOING LIFE BETTER

LOGAN STOUT

NEW YORK

LONDON • NASHVILLE • MELBOURNE • VANCOUVER

GRIT FACTOR
15 ATTRIBUTES FOR DOING LIFE BETTER

Published in New York, New York, by Morgan James Publishing. Morgan James is a trademark of Morgan James, LLC. www.MorganJamesPublishing.com

ISBN 978-1-64279-947-7 paperback
ISBN 978-1-64279-948-4 eBook
Library of Congress Control Number: 2019921213

Cover Design by:
Rachel Lopez
www.r2cdesign.com

Morgan James is a proud partner of Habitat for Humanity Peninsula and Greater Williamsburg. Partners in building since 2006.

Get involved today! Visit
www.MorganJamesBuilds.com

This Book is Dedicated to—

Haley, Miles, and Cooper:

The three of you fuel, support, and inspire me beyond words, and I am honored and humbled. Every second I'm away from you hurts, but we can't change the world from our house!

The Logan Stout Team:

Without you all and your commitment to excellence, this book would not be as powerful as it is, and my vision for these pages would never have been realized. Just like LoganStout.com and the events, courses, content, and materials we provide people every day, *The Grit Factor* will truly add value to the lives of millions of people. Thank you all for your contributions.

My friends and family:

As I started to write each name, I feared that I'd accidentally leave someone off. So I am trusting you all know who you are! And I also trust you know that your love and loyalty mean more to me than I could ever express. "Thank you" doesn't say enough.

TABLE OF CONTENTS

FOREWORD

I have a theory, and I really believe it. I believe your worst weakness can become your single greatest strength. And I think Logan Stout believes that too.

I first met Logan when I was speaking at an event in Dallas, and we connected immediately. He was authentic, and we had a lot in common. We both started from almost nothing: what we have today we earned with hard work and grit. And we both overcame incredible odds to do so.

Today I'm a shark on ABC's hit show *Shark Tank*, but most people don't know my story. I failed at *twenty-two* jobs before landing the only job that would make me happy: I started my own business.

Taking charge of my life, I became an entrepreneur. I would be my own boss, and I was very excited! I borrowed $1,000 from a boyfriend, quit my job as a diner waitress, and used that money to start a tiny real estate business in New York City.

This book is all about how to survive and thrive as an entrepreneur. When I started my business, I was up against thousands of competitors, and I struggled to make it big. But with the help of the unconventional lessons my mom taught me, I built my company into a $6 billion business! To put it in Logan's words, I succeeded because I had a high Grit Factor, and others didn't.

Success is never mystical or magical, and it's never random. Instead, a person's success is quite predictable because of one specific clue. Whether I'm hiring a real estate agent or choosing to invest in a new business owner on *Shark Tank*, I'm always searching for the same quality: a high Grit Factor! I've seen that most people simply don't have what it takes to finish strong. They just quit—and then they blame everything and everyone else for why things didn't work out.

But here's what I know: failure and success are two sides of the same coin, so you can't have one without the other. First comes failure, then comes more failure, then—finally—success. Few people hang in there, though. They fail to stick with a project long enough to achieve success. Grit makes the difference.

Logan Stout's "15 Attributes of Grit" is a recipe for anyone looking to develop their grit. Whether you're an athlete, entrepreneur, sales agent, entertainer, or even a diner waitress like me, Logan's strategy for success will work for you.

Both Logan and I love to win, and we don't stop short of winning. But my true passion is helping other people be their best, and Logan shares this passion. As a people-helper, he offers *Grit Factor* and the truth about what it *really* takes to win!

Enjoy!

Barbara Corcoran

INTRODUCTION

As I've traveled the world speaking, mentoring, and simply meeting people, one thing has become abundantly clear: people everywhere want to do life better! So many people I meet want more out of life. They want to do better for themselves, for their families, and for everyone else who's counting on them—and they don't understand why they can't make "better" happen.

What gives? Why do so many of us feel we're falling short of our true capabilities? And what is missing that might solve this universal human problem? What might help us achieve more? What steps can we take to do life better?

Motivational speakers, doctors, philosophers, sports figures—people from pretty much any field or profession—offer their secret to success. A while ago I did the same thing in my book *Stout Advice: Secrets to Building Yourself, People, and Teams*. Soon to be on its third edition, *Stout Advice* is a quick and valuable read for people wanting to build a firm foundation for success. Now, in these pages, I offer a deeper truth about success.

Our God-Given Potential

I am honored to know some of the world's most successful people—billionaires, celebrities, singers, authors, speakers, Hall of Fame athletes, and others willing to share a wealth of knowledge and experiences. As I've gotten to know these amazing individuals, I've realized that although they are quite different from one another, they do have one essential trait in common. This characteristic means the difference between them being a regular person and being a person who everyone knows, a person whose books we read, movies we watch, songs we listen to, and businesses we patronize. And I call that trait *grit* and this book, *Grit Factor*. In the early chapters, I'll set the stage for our discussion of my 15 Attributes of Grit. Specifically, I'll define success and address conquering whatever is holding us back from achieving it. We'll also look at what grit *isn't* and what it is. *Grit Factor* lays out what I've spent most of my life seeking to teach and help people understand. In these pages I present the substance I believe we all are looking for. The substance we need to go from wanting to conquering.

I gained these insights during years of research and countless experiences helping people be the absolute best version of themselves. You see, I believe—100 percent and with all my heart—that personal development liberates human beings to reach their God-given potential. Call it personal development, personal growth, self-awareness, or something else, but I've come to recognize one absolute difference between those people who *do* and those who *do not* reach that potential, between those who cross the finish line and those who quit, those who climb Success Mountain and those who fall down at the bottom and wonder, *Why not me?* In this book I call this one difference your *Grit Factor*. It is this grit that bridges the gap from where you are to where you want to be! This grit is key to your success.

Logan Stout

SECTION I

THE GRIT FACTOR

Chapter 1

WILL YOU TAKE THE LEAP?

Success comes from knowing that you did your best to become the best that you are capable of becoming.
—John Wooden

T hink about it. What's your personal best when it comes to keeping your New Year's resolutions? Most of us fall off our New Year's resolution bandwagon pretty quickly—many within seven days of the new year! Yet next year, as the New Year's Eve party ends, we're wondering, *Let's see if this will be the year I stick with it.*

Trust me, I've never been great at keeping my New Year's resolutions. In fact, more times than I'd like to admit, I've realized that my New Year's goals are the *exact same* goals I set for myself the year before. And, yes, in the moment I feel a little deflated and a little defeated.

Whatever your specific New Year's resolutions tend to be, I can say with confidence that we all share two goals:

We want to be successful.

We want to be happy.

These resolutions seem simple enough. Why are they so hard to attain?

Living or Existing?

Studies show that key to happiness is actual, measurable progress. If we are getting a little bit better each day, we will experience at least some happiness.

So, if *progress*—as opposed to the actual achievement of a goal—is key to happiness, why do most of us quit along the way?

I think the reason is, most of us are merely *existing*. We are *drifting* through life instead of *intentionally designing* our lives. We may even have uploaded someone else's dream into our heads rather than choosing a path that reflects who we are and what we want out of life.

Or perhaps you've had a sense that something is missing in your life although you can't quite figure out what that something might be. Maybe you feel you could be pursuing something bigger and that you're capable of doing more than you're doing now. I talk to people all the time who say, "Logan, I'm better than this, but I can't seem to get where I want to go!" They can't bridge that gap.

Or maybe you're feeling beat up by life. You've tried so many times that you've quit trying. After falling down over and over again, you've quit dreaming. You may even have concluded that success is possible only for other people, but not for you.

However much you're satisfied or dissatisfied with life right now, here's what I can tell you: You were put on this earth for success! You are not on this earth to simply watch the game of life, to just play along, to merely go through the motions. You are here to change the game! You are here to be a game changer not only for yourself, but for everyone who's counting on you.

I have a great wife and two awesome sons counting on me, and I want to be the best version of *me* for them. And for my employees… for the kids I coach in baseball… for my Dallas Patriots baseball organization… and for God who has given me countless opportunities to be His light in this world. And if I'm going to be the best I can be, and if you are going to be the best you can be, we must rely on and keep strengthening our Grit Factor.

We All Began as Dreamers

When I was a young boy, we—my mom, my brother, and I—lived in a small two-bedroom apartment just outside Dallas. We didn't have much, and my mom worked hard to feed her growing boys. My father wasn't around much after my parents divorced, but I have an amazing relationship with him today. In fact, I've included an immense amount of his knowledge and expertise in LoganStout.com offerings. He has truly been an inspiration in my life. But my mom, her mom, her dad, and eventually my stepdad raised my younger brother and me.

Throughout my childhood, I watched Mom selflessly and always put her boys first. I remember seeing that she was completely drained and wondering how—or if—she was going to keep going, but *she did!* She was dedicated and willing to do whatever it took to give her sons every chance for a bright future. She had grit.

One time, though, when I was twelve years old, I walked into a room and saw my mom with tears in her eyes. The second she noticed I was there, she tried to hide them. When I asked what was wrong, she denied anything was. She never wanted my brother or me to worry about her. She was tough. I began to walk out of the room, but then turned to her and said, "I'm going to take care of you, Mom. I will be wealthy one day, and I promise you, I'll take care of you!"

Yes, as a young boy watching my mother's selflessness, I decided I was going to make money one day. I started dreaming of a better future for our family. I didn't know how it would happen, but I knew I'd stop at nothing. I knew I'd do whatever it took to achieve my dream and help my mom.

As kids, we all dream. Over the years, as I've traveled the world speaking to audiences large and small, or even when I speak to my Dallas Patriots baseball teams, I love bringing young kids on stage and asking, "What do you want to be when you grow up?" Their answers always make me smile. *Professional baseball player*! *Doctor*! *Veterinarian*! Their dreams are big and bold! I've never heard a child say, *I want to work hard at job I hate that barely pays me enough to cover rent!*

In 2017, a shocking study revealed that at least 75 percent of Americans live paycheck to paycheck at some point during the year. What happened to their big, bold, beautiful dreams? What happened?

What Stands Between You and Success

Imagine standing on the edge of a cliff, looking first at the deep and seemingly unbridgeable abyss and then to the other side and then back at the abyss. To get across to the other side will require a real leap, not simply an extra-long step. To try, you'll be stepping far outside your comfort zone, but your dreams will become reality only if you leap to the other side. That's where you'll find success.

As you weigh the decision, you notice what's on your side of the abyss: past failures… current problems… ongoing hardships… unhealthy habits… character flaws… some toxic friendships… suffering family members looking to you for help… excuses… and your untapped God-given potential. Yet this side of the abyss is familiar and therefore comfortable despite how uncomfortable these circumstances make you.

Now consider what opportunities and possibilities await on the other side of the chasm: success... freedom from anything and everything holding you back... a fresh start... a vibrant life... safety and security for your family... work—paid or volunteer—that is significant... a solid financial plan... wealth to share with people in need... and the joy and satisfaction of tapping into your God-given potential. You see all this on the other side. It's beyond your reach, but not beyond a leap of faith.

Will you take the leap?

Chapter 2
WHAT GRIT IS *NOT*

Those who are blessed with the most talent don't necessarily outperform everyone else. It's the people with follow-through who excel.

—Mary Kay Ash

At several points in our life, everyone faces the abyss between *where we are* and *where we want to be*. We all want to get to the other side. We all have dreams. And we all want to be successful! But so few of us make it. Why?

Before I answer that critical question, let me define *success* because my definition is different from most people's.

Success *is reaching your God-given potential in all six aspects of life: mental, physical, financial, relational, emotional, and spiritual.*

To cross the chasm, to be able to reach your God-given potential, and to become *successful* in all six aspects of life, you need the right bridge.

And your Grit Factor is that right bridge, the bridge that takes you from *where you are now* to *where you want to be.* All of us have potential for grit, but few of us cultivate it. Grit is the unsexy, unspoken secret of the super-achievers. It's the one common trait I see firsthand in all successful, world-class individuals. These people have also corralled the power of habit.

Force of Habit, Choice of Habit

We human beings are creatures of habit. Some of our habits are good, and some are not.

In 1960 Maxwell Maltz published *Psycho-Cybernetics.* A plastic surgeon by trade, Maltz claimed in his book that we human beings can establish a new habit in 21 days. Since then others have argued that six weeks is more realistic. Still others say that the time required to develop a good habit—and break a bad habit—depends on many factors, like how motivated we are, how difficult the change will be, how ingrained the old habit it, and how much pressure we're feeling to establish a new habit or break an old one.

And what do habits have to do with grit? Glad you asked. The higher your Grit Factor, the more likely you are to have habits that work *for* you instead of *against* you. When grit fuels healthy habits and, in turn, those healthy habits strengthen our grit, we'll get the results we want. In other words, we'll be able to build a bridge across the chasm to success.

Take a look at some of the building process: thoughts lead to actions... actions lead to habits... and habits lead to results. With the right habits, we get the right results.

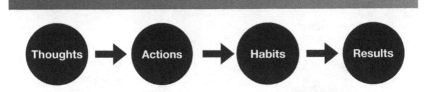

My goal in writing this book is to help you, first, find or reclaim your Grit Factor and then take it to a whole new level. But first I want to make sure you understand what your Grit Factor is... by looking at what it is *not*.

- Your Grit Factor is **not your personality type**. Too often in response to sound counsel, I hear people say, "Oh, that's not my personality." What they really mean is "That's definitely out of my comfort zone!" At certain points in life, all of us have to step outside our comfort zones regardless of our personality type. Name any personality type, and I can give you several examples of people with that kind of personality who stepped outside their comfort zones and crossed the bridge to success. I therefore maintain that personality type has nothing to do with your Grit Factor or with your level of success.

- Your Grit Factor is **not genetics**. Though genes may play a small role in some of the attributes of grit, your Grit Factor is *not* based on genetics. And because of all its parallels to life, I'm going to turn to sports—baseball specifically—to help me make this point. Ivan "Pudge" Rodriguez—one of my best friends—is an example of someone whose Grit Factor overrides the impact of genes. I was honored to be his guest in Cooperstown, New York, when he was inducted into the National Baseball Hall of

Fame: he was only the second catcher in the history of the game to be a first-ballot Hall of Famer. (The other one? The legendary Johnny Bench.)

Logan was a special guest of Ivan "Pudge" Rodriquez at his induction ceremony into the MLB Hall of Fame. Also pictured is Johnny Bench, MLB Hall of Famer. Logan has referred to this picture as the "ultimate baseball sandwich!" (2016)

That picture captures a pretty cool moment for me as I stood between the two greatest catchers in the history of Major League Baseball! Standing at just under five foot eleven next to Pudge, I realized that the height gene—actually, the lack thereof—had nothing to do with why he's one of the greatest catchers of all time. What do Johnny Bench and Pudge Rodriguez have in common? Grit!

Now let me share a more personal example that involves the Dallas Patriots (DallasPatriots.com), one of the world's largest private baseball organizations for kids and an organization I had the joy of establishing. Every summer we hold tryouts that are open to anyone ages five to eighteen. Afterward, we sort through thousands of kids—and it's not always the tallest or the biggest kids who make the team. Nor is it always the strongest or the fastest. As the peddler in Walt Disney's *Aladdin* said about the lamp, "Do not be fooled by its commonplace appearance. Like so many things, it is not what is outside, but what is inside that counts."

So, after we see that a kid's baseball skills qualify him for a Dallas Patriots team, we start looking for character traits like attitude, effort, and focus. I consider traits like those—none of which are genetic—to be the prospective player's *Grit Factor*. And that Grit Factor has led Dallas Patriots grads to good places: as it turns out, every player who has graduated from our Patriots program has been given an opportunity to play college baseball, and every year we have Dallas Patriots players selected during the Major League Baseball draft as well.

Looking back on the thousands of players who have come through the Dallas Patriots organization, I've seen that those who went on to have exceptional careers had basic abilities, yes, but they also had the Grit Factor.

- Your Grit Factor is **not your family name**. As Orison Swett Marden, founder of *Success* magazine, said: "There is no open door to the temple of success. Everyone who enters must make his own door, which closes behind him to all others, not even permitting his own children to pass."

You must make your own door, as I did and as every successful person does. Your parents can't do it for you. My sons, Miles and Cooper, will have to make their own way. They'll have to cross bridges that they build using their Grit Factor. I can't do it for them. And, believe me, having the last name *Stout* won't help them get where they want to be. But their family name has nothing to do with their future success or their Grit Factor. We parents, however, can certainly do things that either strengthen or sabotage our children's Grit Factor. (Teachers, coaches, and other important people in a kid's life can do the same thing.)

Just about every single day, Haley and I have the opportunity to encourage the growth of our sons' grit. When they were younger, for example, every time they asked me to help them put on their shoes, I'd say, "You can do it!" In the beginning, they would reply, "No, I can't, Dad. I tried. I can't do it!" Even though I really wanted to help them, I'd say, "I know you can do it. I believe in you! You got this, buddy!" Sure enough, minutes later Miles or Cooper would come walking up to me with his shoes on. "Look, Daddy! I did it!" I'd smile and say, "I never had a doubt, my man!" Eventually they stopped asking me to help them get dressed. They knew they would figure it out. And when they did, their Grit Factor increased.

- Your Grit Factor is **not your education**. Here are just a few of the many individuals with almost no education who achieved phenomenal success:
  - o Walt Disney dropped out of school at age sixteen. Yet he had the grit to overcome being told no 302 different times by 302 banks that did not want to finance his *crazy* idea: Disneyland.
  - o Billionaire founder of the Virgin Group, Richard Branson dropped out of school at fifteen. Despite fourteen of his start-ups going bust, Branson is one of the greatest successes of this era.
  - o Winston Churchill failed his college entrance exam three times before finally passing. Later he said, "Success is not final, failure is not fatal: it is the courage to continue that counts." And he showed inspiring grit when he stood

up against Nazi Germany, the greatest evil of the last hundred years!

o Thomas Edison had just three months of formal education. Clearly, lack of education did not keep Edison from succeeding. Edison revealed his legendary Grit Factor when, after one thousand attempts, he successfully invented the light bulb.

You yourself may even know people who are half as educated as you are but are making twice as much money. These individuals prove that Grit Factor is not related to education!

One of my business partners is billionaire Darwin Deason. He grew up in The-Middle-of-Nowhere, Arkansas, and then borrowed a few bucks to move to the (relatively) big city of Tulsa, Oklahoma. Long story short, Darwin started a company called ACS that he later sold to Xerox for $6.4 billion. I can assure you that far more educated people who grew up in much more auspicious surroundings than Darwin are flat-out broke. Why was Darwin able to succeed? Grit!

- Your Grit Factor is **not your talent**, as writer John Maxwell makes clear in *Beyond Talent*. (If you haven't read it, do!) In the chapter "Perseverance Sustains Your Talent," Maxwell writes, "Perseverance means stopping not because you're tired, but because the task is done." Too many talented people quit every day before the task is done—and I can't help but think, *What a waste of talent!* As the famous entrepreneur Mary Kay Ash said, "Those who are blessed with the most talent don't necessarily outperform everyone else. It's the people with follow-through who excel." She's right: success takes more than talent. In the simpler words of NBA star Kevin Durant: "Hard work beats talent when talent doesn't work hard."

And—I paraphrase—our Grit Factor beats talent when talent isn't accompanied by grit.

Many of you know of NBA Hall of Famer and global icon Shaquille O'Neal. One day when Shaq was sitting in my office, I asked him about his high-school basketball career. I asked because basketball was my strongest sport. (Hey, I was the two-time district MVP at J. J. Pearce High School! And, yes, I was comparing high-school basketball careers with the one and only Shaq!)

"What kind of player were you in high school?" I asked.

His reply shocked both me and another buddy who was sitting in my office at the time: three-time Super Bowl champion and first-ballot Hall of Fame quarterback Troy Aikman.

"I got cut from my high school basketball team," Shaq said. "I was terrible!"

Troy and I looked at each other. We were speechless. Thinking he might have had a late growth spurt or something, I asked Shaq how tall he was in high school. Shaq said, "I was about seven feet tall, but I couldn't play at all!"

Wow! Talent really isn't the X-factor. Grit is!

Troy then shared how he had to transfer from the University of Oklahoma (he broke an ankle, and during his recovery time Oklahoma changed to the wishbone offense) to UCLA and an offense where he could pass the ball more. Troy also told us about his nightmarish rookie year with the Dallas Cowboys: he finished with a 0-11 record as a starter. His grit, however, ultimately led Troy Aikman to an incredible football career.

And I have one more story of grit that complemented incredible talent.

When I had the privilege of meeting Carrie Underwood, it hit me that her amazing voice would have gone completely unheard if she hadn't tried out for the hit show *American Idol* even after she had put her singing career on hold to pursue a more sensible career in broadcast journalism. But during her senior year of college, she decided to give her dream another shot and tried out for *Idol.* She made the cut, and the show ultimately gave Carrie a platform that allows people around the world to enjoy her talent. She could have easily given up and settled, but her Grit Factor wouldn't let her!

Shaquille O'Neal, Troy Aikman, and Carrie Underwood all have an insane amount of grit that, supplementing their talent, propelled them to global fame. Other individuals have also successfully supplemented their talent with grit. Even though they're not in the spotlight, their grit is remarkable. And yours can be too.

Chapter 3

AND WHAT GRIT *IS*

Most people have uphill dreams, but they have downhill habits. You can't go uphill with downhill habits.
—John C. Maxwell

Why do some people reach their goals in life and others don't? I think one basic difference is this: people who succeed know what they want and what they don't want.

This book gives you an opportunity to define your dreams as well as encouragement and practical suggestions for achieving those dreams. Both steps take a certain amount of grit, but especially the second. When you finish this book, you will have a systematic and focused approach to dominating life!

So have you decided what you want in life? As I go around the country and speak to thousands of people, I see that many people haven't set clear targets for their lives. They have no goals. They have no *bullseye* to even aim at! Or if they finally do decide on what they want out of life, they quickly doubt themselves and often change their minds.

If that sounds like you—or if you've ever struggled to know what you want—then the Bullseye Exercise in this chapter will be an absolute game changer. (Let me assure that the Bullseye Exercise works. It is exactly what I used—and continue to use—to hit target after target. To put it simply, this is how I get results.) And if you do know what you want but haven't been able to achieve it, this training will be an absolute game changer for you as well.

But before you start the Bullseye Exercise, I want to lay out some foundational facts for you.

#1. The mind is a *goal-achieving machine.*

I'm guessing this has happened to you: I lose something (my keys or my phone) and have no idea where it is. I start doing some activity completely unrelated to the missing item, and suddenly the location of the lost item pops into my head! While I wasn't thinking about it, my subconscious mind was busy doing the searching for me! It's amazing!

Here's another example of how amazingly our brains work. You decide you want to buy a new car. As you drive it off the lot, you think it's one of a kind. After all, the dealer told you it was. But suddenly you start seeing your exact car everywhere! They were there all along, but until you gave your mind that target, you never noticed those cars.

I could go on with examples. The point is, your mind is an incredible, powerful, God-given tool that achieves goals on our behalf… once it has a clear target. Once it has a bullseye! Important note: You will never hit a bullseye that doesn't exist. You may be the greatest sniper of all time, but you still need a target.

#2. Your bullseyes must *excite* you!

First off, be sure these bullseyes are *your* dreams, *your* visions of a better life. The purpose here is for you to establish *your* bullseyes. These aren't to be your parents' dreams. Or your spouse's. These dreams are *yours*.

Your bullseyes must be *compelling*. They must be so exciting that you wake up with fire in your belly, excited and eager to pursue them! And if you're going to dream, go ahead and dream big and bold! It takes the same amount of time to dream big as it does to dream small, so dream big!

Next, your bullseyes should *benefit* those you love. Thinking about everyone who will benefit once you've hit your bullseyes will add fuel to your fire!

#3. You must *believe* you can achieve your bullseyes.

Yes, your bullseyes must be big and bold, but not so big that you can't hit them. For example, let's say your financial bullseye is having a trillion dollars in the bank. That's definitely big and bold, but, realistically, do you believe you can achieve it? Probably not. And because you don't believe you can achieve it, you'll never put in the necessary effort to reach that goal, or your effort will be short-lived. So find your sweet spot: set a goal that excites you and that you *believe* you can achieve! That's the bullseye!

#4. Your bullseyes *will grow* bigger and bolder as you grow.

As you start to develop the attributes that we talk about in this book, your abilities will grow, so your bullseyes will grow as well. In other words, the more you chase your current dreams, the bigger your dreams will become. That's one of the beautiful things about pursuing your dreams!

An example will probably be helpful. Let's imagine right now your weight-loss goal is ten pounds even though you really need to lose twenty-five pounds. As you get closer and closer to your initial goal of losing ten pounds, you start to think bigger. Your bullseye changes from losing ten pounds to losing twenty-five pounds. Before long, you've lost all the weight you needed to, and now you're focused on building muscle.

#5. Your bullseyes need your *daily* attention.

To set a bullseye only to never look at it again will do you no good! I strongly encourage you to look at your bullseyes daily! Or two times a day. Once in the morning; once at night. We want to keep our bullseyes in the forefront of our minds all the time.

That's why, in this book, I've provided you with templates and worksheets for creating bullseyes for your life. You can use the forms at the end of this chapter, or you can create your own. Either way, post your bullseyes so you will see them every day. Maybe on the mirror in your bathroom or on the door of your refrigerator. Perhaps put them on your smartphone or use the list as a screen saver. You decide where. Know it's important for all of us—myself included—to review our bullseyes on a daily basis.

#6. You need a bullseye for *every aspect* of your life.

The six aspects of life are mental, physical, spiritual, financial, emotional, and relational. After you finish reading this chapter, you're going to set at least one bullseye for each aspect. For some aspects you may want multiple bullseyes. For instance, in the relational aspect, you may want to set a bullseye for your spouse as well as ones for your kid(s), boss, coach, or whomever.

A quick aside. Based on personal experience I can tell you that if you're weak in any one of these six aspects, the other five will suffer. If you're weak emotionally, for instance, your body suffers physically. If you're weak financially, your relationships are strained by finances. Each of the six affects the other five. Even if you have one or two aspects of your life in a fairly healthy place, the other weaker parts of your life will eventually bring down those healthier ones.

Again, in a few minutes, you're going to set at least one bullseye for each aspect of your life, so you'll have a minimum of six bullseyes to work toward.

#7. You're *never stagnant.*

You're either getting better, or you're getting worse. You're either getting closer to reaching your bullseye, or you're getting further away. There is no staying the same! That's just not how life works!

Consider, for instance, a Physical Bullseye. If you're not exercising, your body is naturally getting weaker. If you're not actively working to improve your relationships, they will suffer as well. This principle applies to all six aspects of life: you are never stagnant.

#8. *Habits* are key.

I do think the most practical way you can raise your Grit Factor is to replace bad habits with the best habits. When you do, you'll hit your bullseye for every aspect of life. Remember, when we struggle with one attribute, our struggling drags down our scores in other attributes of grit. For example, if your marriage is on the rocks, that reality will impact other areas of your life.

Second, our habits can greatly influence our performance in life, and grit can help us identify and break our downhill habits. You'll then be freer to pursue your uphill dreams. Grit definitely makes the difference between those who *do* and those who *do not*, between those who *have* and those who *have not*. Grit is the habit of champions!

Let's think for a minute about our habits. As I've said, we're either getting better or we're getting worse, and our habits significantly influence which option we're choosing, intentionally or by default! Simply put, our habits are either serving us or sabotaging us. They're either moving us toward our bullseyes, or they're pulling us in the opposite direction.

The John Maxwell quote that opens this chapter is spot-on: "Most people have uphill dreams, but downhill habits." Those downhill habits sabotage dreams, derail progress toward goals, and distract us from our bullseyes. Downhill habits are leaks in their boat. It's just a matter of time before it sinks!

Meanwhile, successful people have uphill habits that move them toward the fulfillment of their goals and the realization of their dreams. Their habits serve them well by taking them, step-by-step, closer to their bullseyes. Habits help, but there's nothing automatic about reaching your goals. As Maxwell puts it, "You intentionally have to turn downhill sliding into uphill climbing." The key word there is *intentionally*. It's no accident that successful people have successful habits. Success happens by design!

That's why your bullseye sheets have places where you can write down both your Downhill Habits and your Uphill Habits. Hitting your bullseyes in all aspects of life is simple but not easy. The simple part is understanding the need to replace negative Downhill Habits with positive Uphill ones. Such habits, though, are rarely easy to break—but *all* are breakable. That may be worth repeating: *all* your habits are breakable. You can do it! It's not always easy, but your efforts to break your Downhill Habit will be 100 percent worth whatever energy you invest!

In addition to positive habits, the skill of observation is helpful because—as motivational speaker Jim Rohn says, "Success leaves clues." The problem is, the average person isn't around enough successful people on a day-to-day basis to be able to look for and find those clues. Unable to see how highly successful people actually live their daily lives, that person is left somewhat mystified as to what success looks like and what becoming successful requires. Fortunately, I have lived—and I continue to live—next to some greats. So I can confirm that success does leave clues. I've been able to observe these successful people, recognize those clues, apply them to my life, and now share them in *The Grit Factor*.

Defining Your Targets

On the next several pages, I've provided a bullseye for each aspect of life: Mental, Emotional, Relational, Physical, Spiritual, and Financial. Each page—as I mentioned—has places to list some Uphill Habits and some Downhill Habits. The goal is for all of us is to replace our bad habits with the best habits. Our goal is a systematic approach to raising your Grit Factor and thereby improving all six aspects of your life.

An important note: We tend to spend more time on the tangible aspects of life, such as Money and Physical Health. But it's the intangible aspects of life that make the tangible possible and meaningful! Granted, each aspect of life has its tangible *and* intangible elements. But in general, intangible thoughts lead to actions, actions lead to habits, and habits lead to results. So if we don't have the right thoughts, then our actions, habits, and results will not be anything close to what they could be! So be sure to invest as much time on the Mental, Emotional, Spiritual, and Relational aspects of life as you do in the Physical and Financial aspects. Maybe even more time!

Now, with the foundational facts laid out and my pep talk behind us, let's get you started on spelling out your goals. Don't hurry through the following Bullseye Exercises. Also, as you make it a priority to review them every day, feel free to update them when you do. Those updates will reflect your change from Downhill Habits to Uphill ones that move you toward success. At the end of this chapter you will find The Bullseye

Exercise worksheet provided for you to enter your goals in each of the six aspects of your life. Since you now know that each aspect works together, I hope this will help you track your success or areas of weakness.

BULLSEYE EXERCISE: MENTAL

What do you want? In what specific ways do you want to grow mentally? *Write that next to Mental Bullseye below. That's your bullseye!* (Example: be a better leader)

What Downhill Habits might be sabotaging your progress toward your mental goal(s)? *List those below under "Downhill Habits."* (Examples: watching late-night talk-shows; listening to sports radio on my morning commute)

What Uphill Habits will help you hit your mental bullseye(s)? *List under "Uphill Habits."* (Examples: watch a YouTube video related to personal growth every evening; listen to a leadership audiobook on my morning commute)

◎ MENTAL BULLSEYE: _____

DOWNHILL HABITS: UPHILL HABITS:

_____   _____

_____   _____

_____   _____

_____   _____

_____   _____

BULLSEYE EXERCISE: PHYSICAL

What do you want? In what specific ways do you want to grow physically? *Write that that next to Physical Bullseye below. That's your bullseye!* (Example: lose fifteen pounds)

What Downhill Habits might be sabotaging your progress toward your physical goal(s)? *List under "Downhill Habits."* (Examples: the bagel and cream cheese I have every morning; my fast-food lunches)

What Uphill Habits will help you hit your physical bullseye(s)? *List under "Uphill Habits."* (Examples: have a healthy smoothie for breakfast; journal what I eat every day)

◎ PHYSICAL BULLSEYE: _____

DOWNHILL HABITS: UPHILL HABITS:

_____   _____

_____   _____

_____   _____

_____   _____

_____   _____

BULLSEYE EXERCISE: SPIRITUAL

What do you want? In what specific ways do you want to grow spiritually? *Write that that next to Spiritual Bullseye below. That's your bullseye!* (Example: improve my relationship with God)

What Downhill Habits might be sabotaging your progress toward your spiritual goal(s)? *List under "Downhill Habits."* (Examples: staying out so late Saturday night that I'm tired at church on Sunday; waking up late on workdays and having no time to read the Bible in the morning)

What Uphill Habits will help you hit your spiritual bullseye(s)? *List under "Uphill Habits."* (Examples: read a devotional book for ten minutes every morning; pray with my spouse and with my kids every night)

◎ SPIRITUAL BULLSEYE: _____

DOWNHILL HABITS: UPHILL HABITS:

_____   _____

_____   _____

_____   _____

_____   _____

_____   _____

BULLSEYE EXERCISE: FINANCIAL

What do you want? In what specific ways do you want to grow financially? *Write that next to Financial Bullseye below. That's your bullseye!* (Example: earn $2,000 more a month)

What Downhill Habits might be sabotaging your progress toward your financial goal(s)? *List under "Downhill Habits."* (Examples: eating out too often; watching a lot of TV)

What Uphill Habits will help you hit your financial bullseye(s)? *List under "Uphill Habits."* (Examples: take my lunch to work; stop buying what I don't need [pricey shoes, cool golf clubs]; network for supplemental job)

◎ FINANCIAL BULLSEYE: _____

DOWNHILL HABITS: UPHILL HABITS:

_____   _____

_____   _____

_____   _____

_____   _____

_____   _____

BULLSEYE EXERCISE: EMOTIONAL

What do you want? In what specific ways do you want to grow emotionally? *Write that next to Emotional Bullseye below. That's your bullseye!* (Example: increase my emotional strength)

What Downhill Habits might be sabotaging your progress toward your emotional goal(s)? *List under "Downhill Habits."* (Examples: staying in my comfort zone; showing frustration; being hot-tempered)

What Uphill Habits will help you hit your emotional bullseye(s)? *List under "Uphill Habits."* (Examples: every day do one thing that scares me; evaluate moments that frustrated me each day and how I responded)

◎ EMOTIONAL BULLSEYE: _____

DOWNHILL HABITS: UPHILL HABITS:

_____   _____

_____   _____

_____   _____

_____   _____

_____   _____

BULLSEYE EXERCISE: RELATIONAL

What do you want? In what specific ways do you want to grow relationally? *Write that next to Relational Bullseye below. That's your bullseye!* (Example: vibrant and growing relationships with my spouse and kids)

What Downhill Habits might be sabotaging your progress toward your relationship goal(s)? *List under "Downhill Habits."* (Examples: having the TV on and cellphones at the table during dinnertime; spending too much time looking at my phone instead of being present when I'm with family and friends)

What Uphill Habits will help you hit your relationship bullseye(s)? *List under "Uphill Habits."* (Examples: a weekly date night with my spouse; showing up for all my kids' games)

◎ RELATIONAL BULLSEYE: _____

DOWNHILL HABITS: UPHILL HABITS:

_____   _____

_____   _____

_____   _____

_____   _____

_____   _____

Be sure to revisit each bullseye after reading about an attribute of grit in the second part of this book. I also refer to these grit attributes as *traits of the super-achievers* because these individuals do have a high Grit Factor. We're going to dive into each one.

And a word of encouragement. This book is like anything else in life: the more you put into it, the more you will get out of it. In other words, this book will help you grow as much as you allow it to.

Chapter 4

CAN GRIT GROW?

If you want something you've never had, you've got to do something you've never done.

—Thomas Jefferson

B efore we get into the meat of the book, I want to address one of the biggest questions about grit: "Can we really improve our Grit Factor? Can we actually grow grit?"

To answer those questions, we first need to understand that grit is a behavior. If grit were a personality trait, the change from gritty to grittier would be more difficult. But look at these words and phrases that are synonymous with grit: *courage, bravery, backbone, spirit, strength of character, strength of will, moral fiber, nerve, fortitude, toughness, hardiness, resolve, resolution, determination, tenacity, perseverance,* and *endurance.* Now look again at that list and consider the behavior implied by each word or phrase. Can you now accept that grit is a behavior? If so, we must next agree that behaviors can change. If you believe—as I do—that we can change our behavior, then we also agree that we can grow gritty behaviors and become grittier.

How to Measure Your Grit Factor

I've learned that top-performing leaders in every walk of life are willing to identify, own, and deal with their counterproductive behaviors. They're willing to be vulnerable, to change, and to grow. They're willing to be the kind of leader we all want to follow. Are you willing to identify and eliminate your counterproductive behaviors and become grittier so that you can hit your goals, have more fun, and earn more?

When I consider becoming grittier, I think of The Flippen group, a dynamic organization that has been working for more than 25 years to "bring out the best in you, your team, and your organization."

The Flippen Profile lists behavior scale measurements: Endurance Scale, Urgency & Intensity Scale, and Self-Confidence Scale. (Interestingly, the names of these scales incorporate all the words listed as synonyms of *grit*.) Rather than being subjective, The Flippen Profile focuses solely on the behaviors of a gritty person. I scored very high on my grit scales. (I'm relaying the data because it gives me—and this book—greater credibility.)

So it's great for me to see I have a high Grit Factor, but I've realized that sometimes I can push too hard. You might wonder, *how can someone be too gritty?* Well, at times I can push too hard and refuse to give in when moving on would be the right decision. And that's the coolest thing I learned about myself from the Flippen Profile.

At other times, I can even overplay some of my strengths. For example, my confidence can be misunderstood as arrogance. My urgency and intensity can demoralize people when I'm not careful to moderate those traits. I see this happen just about every season when I coach kids in baseball. At times I realize I was too hard on the players, and when I do, I set a team meeting and apologize.

I share these specifics about my Flippen Profile for a specific reason. I want you to remember that not one of us human beings is perfect. People don't expect us to be perfect. They expect us to be authentic, not perfect.

Looking in the Mirror

Why do our Endurance Scale, Urgency & Intensity Scale, and Self-Confidence Scale matter? Because they provide a baseline for us: we can know our starting point, and we can assess our growth. It's an exciting reality that we can grow in grittiness! If I'm not happy about what the scales reveal, then I'll want a growth plan that would help me increase my grittiness.

According to Webster's, *Endurance* is "the ability to withstand hardship or adversity; especially, the ability to sustain a prolonged stressful effort or activity." High scorers in this category know how to persevere. Rather than surrender, they keep forging ahead despite the difficulty. Low scorers tend to let go of a challenging task more quickly. They may be indifferent or apathetic about their assignments, and they may show a lack of follow-through.

Our score on the scale of *Urgency & Intensity* indicates the value we place on time. High scorers are noticeably focused on completing a given task, and they generally enjoy being recognized for their accomplishments. Placing a high value on time, they tend to move through life faster than most people. High scorers are typically more goal-directed and even impatient, while low scorers are more relaxed and approachable. Low scorers may still be very driven, but the need to achieve may not be their primary motivation.

Where you fall on the *Self-Confidence* scale reflects your overall belief in yourself and your abilities. High scorers are self-assured and confident, while low scorers are more likely to second-guess themselves and have difficulty taking risks.

While I encourage you to check out your Flippen Profile at flippenprofile.com, you can simply use these definitions of the three behavioral scales and rate yourself on a scale of 1-10: 0-4 is a low score; 5-7, a mid-range score; and 8-10, a high score. In this self-assessment, you might find it helpful to think about someone you know whom you would rate high in each of these three categories. Who in your life is always on the move, working hard to achieve every day, self-assured, and always reaching a goal or completing an assignment? Although it can serve them well, this bulldog mentality can come across as stubborn and as poor judgment about when to let go. If I just described you, you would measure in that 8-10 range. If you show these behaviors at times, you are more than likely in the midrange. If you lack energy, aren't very driven, struggle to complete tasks, lack motivation, or don't have a strong sense of duty, then you are likely to score lower.

Too Much of a Good Thing

Yes, you read it correctly: too much of a good thing. This statement may seem counterintuitive, but there are risks to being too high—or too low—in these behavioral measurements. When we are trying to become grittier, we will activate those behaviors that reflect an urgency and intensity, a strong belief in ourselves and in our task, and a "get after it" attitude. If, however, you get feedback that you seem to have trouble moving on from what is clearly a futile effort or lost cause, that your perceived stubbornness is off-putting, that you operate at too fast a pace, or that people seem less important to you than tasks, pay attention to that input. Ideally, you want to measure high in these three areas, but be aware of being overbearing and of not moving forward when it's time.

Although most of us are trying to become grittier, we occasionally meet people who may be too gritty. On occasion I've definitely been one of those people. I, for instance, can and often do move at a superfast pace—as my beautiful bride will attest. At times Haley reminds me to slow down and not take on too many projects. I also have a lot of self-confidence, and because of my accomplishments, I have very little doubt that I will achieve whatever I attempt. So, as I mentioned earlier, I need to be careful that I don't come across as arrogant or cocky to people who don't have a strong belief in themselves. I also have great endurance. As a former athlete (although, if you know athletes, we never consider ourselves "former" athletes), I am physically in great shape (so I tell myself). I also have mental and emotional strength that allows me to push through tough times and adversity. Again, I need to be aware of when to let go and not keep pushing, especially not pushing people. My expectations are extremely high, and I know I can wear on people if I'm not careful.

Be Encouraged!

The Grit Factor is necessary if you want to be a game changer. Fully understanding the Grit Factor allows you to connect the dots—to draw a line—between where you are and where you want to be. That path is important. So is having the right core values in life, the right mission statement, the right motives, and the right intentions. But without grit, we would struggle more to reach our goals.

And we must all remember that although the goals and the dreams are free, the journey is not. We all must pay a price to reach our goals and dreams, and the best currency is grit. The higher your Grit Factor, the higher the probability of your success.

Now, I've always said the greatest way to waste time is by trying to control something you have no control over. Or trying to improve something you have no chance of improving. I also believe in the converse: the greatest use of time is to take control of what you *can* control! And here's the great news: *you* control your Grit Factor!

Chapter 5

UNDERSTANDING LIFE'S JOURNEYS: STAGES 1-4

Victorious warriors win first and then go to war, while defeated warriors go to war first and then seek to win.
—Sun Tzu

There I am, relaxed in my seat, flying in comfort thirty thousand feet in the air, when I suddenly hear a slight *bing*, and the Fasten Seat Belt light flashes on. The captain's voice comes over the intercom.

"Ladies and gentlemen, this is your captain speaking," he says calmly. "We have a mild storm just ahead. We can expect a few bumps as we pass through it, so we've turned on the Fasten Seat Belt sign. No big deal. We should be through the storm in just a few minutes. Sit back, relax, and enjoy the flight. Thank you."

Then the flight attendants walk through the aisles, smiling just as broadly as they had when we boarded. "Please take your seat," they

41

instruct a few stray passengers. A few minutes later, the plane starts to shake. I feel the aircraft drop and then be jerked from side to side. When I look around, not many people seem at all bothered by the turmoil. A few passengers are gripping their armrests, but for the most part, everyone is fine. Minutes later, we're through the storm, and the bumpiness is behind us. I hear another slight *bing,* and the Fasten Seat Belt sign is off.

Now imagine with me that the captain gets on the intercom, but you hear an unidentified voice say, "Sit down immediately and fasten your seat belts right now!" Just as he finishes, the plane suddenly drops and then starts moving from side to side. Not knowing anything about why this is happening, the passengers are frightened, some are panicking, and children are crying. Others are promising themselves they'll *never* fly again—if they happen to land safely. Who knows how many silent and urgent prayers for safety would have been uttered as everyone tightened their seat belts and clutched their armrests?

Thankfully, that second scenario is not how our airlines inform passengers about upcoming bumpiness. Captains are trained to protect their crew and passengers. They know they are responsible for the safety and well-being of everyone on the plane. They're taught to communicate calmly and clearly about upcoming turbulence: *It's no big deal. This is normal. We'll only be in the storm a few minutes.* When the passengers board the plane, they entrust themselves to the captain's leadership, and the captain knows that.

Grit or Quit?

So why the airplane story? Because by picking up this book, you've entrusted yourself to my leadership, and I am deeply honored. As your captain, so to speak, I am required to communicate honestly and truthfully. And I do so even if I'm aware you might not like what I have to say. It's my job to lead you from *where you are now* to *where you want to be.* You are giving me the precious gift of your time, something you can never get back. Let me assure you, if you read this book through to the end, do the interactive exercises, and apply these principles, you will live every aspect of your life on an entirely new level. I know this to be true because I've seen thousands and thousands of people apply to their lives the teachings and lessons in this book. I am humbled and gratified to hear the incredible testimonies of individuals, families, teams, and companies all over the world.

Notice I said, "if you read this book through to the end." And I wrote this because I see in our culture that loyalty, commitment, and perseverance are not valued as they once were. Relationships, jobs, and affiliations don't always last long. It's rare, for instance, to see an athlete play on the same team for an extended amount of time. People's job histories on their LinkedIn profiles show that such transience is common in the business world as well. Success takes work *and* time. Not just work. Not just time. My experience suggests that people don't want to work very hard and aren't too willing to put in the time. Rather, they chase shiny object after shiny object and end up joining the world's large population of professional quitters.

I believe there are two fundamental reasons why people quit. First, they don't have proper expectations. The captain—perhaps the parents, maybe the culture at large—never got on the intercom and told them about the turbulence they'd inevitably experience wherever they journey. Second, I believe virtually 99 percent of the population has a low Grit Factor. But this book provides a systematic approach to reaching your goals and dreams by teaching you how to grow your grit. And the higher your Grit Factor, the higher the probability you'll hit your bullseyes.

I'm going to set the scene and help you know what to expect. Yes, this is your captain speaking on the intercom, offering you peace and purpose as you travel to your desired destination. Basically, in your journey, you will encounter five stages.

Going or Growing Through the Process

As I've studied human behavior and done life and business with the most successful people in the world, I've noticed that everyone experiences wins and losses, success and adversity. The most successful people aren't immune to what everyone else *goes* through, but they choose to *grow* through the process—and they don't quit. I've mentored and/or learned from billionaires, Hall of Fame athletes, world-famous entertainers, and others, and here's what I know to be true about their journeys, your journey, and mine: Every life experience we journey through—from start to finish—has five stages. When you get married, you and your spouse go through these five stages. When you start a new job or a new business, you go through five stages. When you first get your real estate license or a gym membership, you go through the same five stages. No matter the journey, it has five stages—unless you quit.

Knowing up front about these stages can help you get through them. In addition, your Grit Factor will help determine your success or failure in each of The Five Stages. A low Grit Factor, however, means a low probability of reaching, much less completing, Stage 5. A high Grit Factor increases the odds of succeeding in Stage 5, the odds of reaching goals and fulfilling dreams. The best part about reaching Stage 5 is that your Grit Factor will have been tested, refined, and grown as you journeyed.

The 5 Stages

Stage 1: Honeymoon

Stage 2: Adversity

Stage 3: Progress

Stage 4: Management Mode

Stage 5: Success

Stage 1: Honeymoon

The beginning of any endeavor is always exciting! New and different can be thrilling and energizing! Some of these glimpses into Stage 1 will be familiar:

- Two people who have just started dating can't seem to keep their hands off each other; stay up until 2 a.m. talking about *absolutely nothing*; and want to be together every moment of every day.
- In the first days and even weeks of a new job, the new hire has a new desk, new coworkers, new clients, and a genuine excitement about adding value to the company.
- The first few days or weeks at the gym or on a diet are energized by a new workout plan, even a new gym, a new approach to eating healthy, a fresh commitment to self-discipline, and the new goal of a new you.
- In real estate, excitement comes with new clients, different opportunities to learn, the first listing, the first sale!
- In sports, the first week of practice and the renewed hope of a championship season fuel the athletes' energy and excitement.

No matter what the journey, no matter what the situation, people in the Honeymoon Stage are enthusiastic! The enthusiasm comes from hope, and hope fuels the enthusiasm. All is good in Stage 1. Very good!

Stage 2: Adversity

Inevitably, the Honeymoon stage will end, and turbulence will come. *Ladies and gentlemen, this is your captain speaking. We have a storm just ahead. Expect a few bumps...*

Inevitably, adversity will come as we journey through life. It always does. So expect it. Not being blindsided by the abrupt and jarring end of the Honeymoon Stage can help us cope with whatever type of adversity—whatever turbulence—we encounter.

- In a marriage, the Adversity Stage begins when we realize we're in a relationship with another imperfect and sinful human being who—on top of that—doesn't put the cap on the toothpaste tube or hang the toilet paper roll "right." On a far more serious note than toothpaste tubes are the turbulence of financial problems, a lost job, difficulties with in-laws, infertility, or a serious medical diagnosis.
- In a new job, the Adversity Stage arrives when issues with your new boss arise, when the coworker's bad attitude seems unbearable, or responsibilities increase significantly but the pay doesn't.
- In sales, turbulence comes with rejection, cold calls that bear no fruit, clients backing out of deals, and people not returning phone calls. And there's no satellite weather picture telling you when the turbulence will end.
- The turbulence of rejection also comes for those of us who start a home-based business! The nicest, sweetest woman I know—and a shoo-in for my first sale—actually responded with "Logan, you're going to go to jail! I can't believe you would be involved in something like this. Have you lost your mind?" Once I convinced her this was a sound business, my mom did become my first customer. So, home-based entrepreneurs, be prepared to face adversity from even your parents! (Fun fact: Home-based businesses—often direct-sales companies—represent more annual revenue than pro football, baseball, basketball, and hockey combined! Having earned millions of dollars in the direct-sales space by the age of twenty-five myself, I can personally confirm that metric.)

- In health and fitness, adversity may come as early as day two when you can hardly get out of bed because you're so sore from your day-one workout. Other forms of adversity in the world of exercise and diet are pulling a muscle you never knew you had; doing everything you're supposed to do to lose weight, but the scale isn't budging; or your child brings home a nasty virus and you're sick for a week. The Honeymoon Stage is definitely over!

- I once read that more than 90 percent of all people with a real estate license never sell a single home! I don't know if that stat is correct today or not, but the point is still relevant: making no sales definitely qualifies as adversity. After driving a client around for months only to learn that the client isn't ready to buy, the new real estate agent thinks, *I've spent a lot of time and money, and I have nothing to show for it!* Adversity!

- The many kids I mentor in the Dallas Patriots select baseball organization also know the transition from honeymoon to adversity. Taking recruiting trips to universities is definitely Honeymoon Stage stuff. But then—sometimes even during their first week of college practices—they encounter turbulence and call me: *Coach Stout, this is a lot harder than I thought it would be! And you were right. The coaches were a lot nicer when they were recruiting me than they are in practice!*

Unexpectedly, people hit by sudden turbulence find themselves at a crossroads: grit or quit?

Talk to anyone who has accomplished anything significant and ask about the adversity they have faced. You may see that the greatness of their achievements is correlated to the amount of adversity they have had to overcome. The same is true for real-life heroes. Think of the obstacles overcome by award-winning singer/songwriter/pianist Stevie Wonder (blind from birth); physicist Stephen Hawking (diagnosed with ALS when he was twenty-one); Helen Keller (the first blind and deaf person to earn a college degree); surfer Bethany Hamilton (world-class surfer even after being attacked by a shark and losing her arm); composer Ludwig van Beethoven (who started losing his hearing when he was 26 and composed most of his works when he was completely deaf); and motivational speaker, husband, and father Nick Vujicic (born without legs or arms).

Yet the Adversity Stage is when many people *quit* either because they didn't know adversity was coming, or (the point of this book) they have a low Grit Factor. You, dear reader, can't claim ignorance. Let me be clear: No matter your endeavor, adversity is coming! In fact, anything worthwhile will take longer, cost more, and have more heartache than you ever imagined. That's one way you know it's worth it!

Stage 3: Progress

People who have any grit at all will reach Stage 3, a milestone indicating progress. And you may not know that studies have revealed that progress is key to happiness. Being a little bit better today than yesterday—and the hope of being a little bit better tomorrow—can make a person happy. When we make progress—when we learn something, sign a new client, bench-press more weight—we feel good. When we go to a leadership event or take a course (maybe you've done one of my online courses, been to one-day live events, and/or attended one of the Leadership Summits we offer at LoganStout.com), we expand not only our minds but also our dreams. And, yes, that gives us happiness and energy. In fact, whenever we expand our lives, we feel good. When we shrink our lives, we feel bad. Progress is definitely expansion.

Progress is also movement toward success, a word that I know means different things to different people. As I said in chapter 2, I believe success is the fulfillment of our God-given potential in six areas of life: Physical, Mental, Spiritual, Financial, Emotional, and Relational.

According to this definition, when we're in the Progress Stage, we're becoming successful. We are headed in the right direction. Adversity is *not* holding us back. There is, however, no finish line when it comes to success. No matter how much you and I grow, there is always room for further growth. And when you grow you, everything around you grows. Growth literally creates the possibility of infinite future growth!

Now, you might think progress or growth becomes a habitual thing, but it doesn't. With progress can come complacency. People don't realize that what got them to this point won't take them to greater heights. For example, a person working out in the gym can't keep doing the same workout every day. Only if they vary their activities and take their workouts to a new level will they see results.

In other words, you have to continue to grow you if you want to grow in all areas of your life. But too many people make progress, enjoy some great short-term results—like a promotion, a pay raise, more influence, or other accolades—and stop growing. Maybe they begin to think they are a lot better than they really are. Then, when other people look to them to lead, they start managing rather than leading people. You would think all is well but managing is very different from leading. These Stage 3 people of progress have entered Stage 4, which I call Management Mode.

Stage 4: Management Mode

Have you ever seen a lion after it has eaten? Sprawled out in the African sun, the beast yawns in contentment. The once aggressive hunter is hungry no more. Now, I think that's a gruesome example (I can't even watch the Discovery Channel because I hate seeing things die), but the lion is a perfect illustration of Stage 4: Management Mode. Intense activity has given way to rest and inactivity.

And that's not just the lion's nature. Unfortunately, it is human nature as well. We make a little progress, we become content, and we stop doing the things that got us to this point of contentment. We no longer focus on what we need to do to reach new levels. We have fallen into Management Mode.

What exactly is Management Mode? We need look no further than businesses such as real estate and insurance for an illustration. A person achieves a certain rank; gains associates, affiliates, and business partners; and starts to manage those teammates. This Stage 3 successful person starts doing conference calls but stops recruiting and going after new sales. This once energetic worker now spends time in front of a computer screen or behind the closed office door rather than being out in the field hunting for new clients. This now-Stage 4 worker barks commands to the team, asks why others aren't producing, and spends time training, coaching, teaching, but not *doing*! Their complacency has stopped their activity and, as a result, their growth. And this is where the greater damage happens. The team sees what the leader does, and that's what they do. The leader brings in new leads, and the team brings

Miles and Cooper learning how to take responsibility and work hard by giving their "mini" Cadillac Escalade a car wash.

in new leads. The leader sits around, and the team sits around. The team follows the leader's example and doing what the Stage 4 leader is doing means doing… nothing.

As parents learn—and businesspeople can learn as well—life is caught, not taught. Case in point. My twin boys love to drive their cars. As I write this book, they are seven years old. (Now you understand the type of cars they're driving.)

Insert #2 pics of Miles and Cooper driving cars

One day the boys refused to drive their cars until they had the keys. I had no clue what they were talking about because their toy cars don't require keys. Even after I informed them of this reality, they refused to drive their cars. When I asked them how they learned about keys, they pointed out that Mommy and Daddy never drive cars without keys. How could they possibly drive their cars without keys! So, yes, we had keys made for them, and now they drive around with keys in their cars!

Followers at work—just like little followers at home—see what we do, and that's what they do… even if it makes zero sense. We leaders need to remember that if we're working hard at our business, our team will work hard at theirs.

Are you still wondering how Stage 4 happens? In part, it happens because the only constant in life is that nothing is constant. Maybe energy wanes or, as I mentioned, we get complacent. But I believe that Management Mode is, at its core, laziness. We get too comfortable and start assuming that others will do the work. Rather than leading by example as we once did, we rest on our laurels. And while we think momentum and a well-established way of doing things will maintain the status quo and business will stay the same…nothing stays the same. When a leader is in Management Mode, then results, revenue, productivity, morale, and other aspects of the business are guaranteed to decrease. After all, things in this world are either growing or dying.

That's why I believe that Management Mode is the beginning of the end. The only way we can stop this decline is to, first, realize we're in Management Mode and, second, get to work earning our way to Stage 5!

Chapter 6
UNDERSTANDING LIFE'S JOURNEYS: STAGE 5

I hated every minute of training, but I said, "Don't quit. Suffer now and live the rest of your life a champion."
—Muhammad Ali

As I wrote in the preceding chapter, I learned from observing people and then I confirmed in my research that we journey through life experiences in five stages. When you get married, you and your spouse go through The 5 Stages. When you start a new job or a new business, you go through The 5 Stages. When you first get your real estate license or a gym membership, you go through the same 5 Stages. No matter the journey, it has 5 Stages—unless you quit. We move from Stage 1: Honeymoon (everything is great!), to Stage 2: Adversity (it's inevitable!), then Stage 3: Progress (choose to *grow* through that adversity), and to Stage 4: Management Mode (beware! you've stopped growing—but don't quit). Now we'll look at Stage 5: Success.

Stage 5: Success

I know you won't be surprised but moving out of Management Mode and into the final stage where we experience Success, takes a very high Grit Factor. Actually, without that high Grit Factor, you would never have persevered through Stages 1-4 to even reach Stage 5. Most people quit somewhere between Stage 2 and Stage 4. But I'm confident you can master all five stages. You see, I've mentored some of the most successful people in the world, and I assure you they are *not* any better than anyone else. They simply have a higher level of grit. Their Grit Factors are truly exceptional!

That said, I've never met anyone who doesn't want to reach his or her full potential. After a few questions, even people who are struggling and in a funk about their lives admit that they, too, want more. We all do! Too many people are living quiet lives of desperation. *There has to be more to life than this!* they think—and they're right! There is more to life than what any of us are currently experiencing. We each have an infinite amount of unlimited potential, and that's why I wrote this book.

My Hero

Now, if you'd told me years ago that I'd be where I am today, doing life with the people I'm doing life with, I would have smiled at your amazing but far-fetched dream. Here's my reality: I was seventeen years old when I read my first leadership book ever: *Developing the Leader Within You* by John C. Maxwell, who is considered the greatest leadership expert in the world. This guy mentors and speaks to the most powerful people in the world, and I wanted to meet him.

I heard that John C. Maxwell was speaking at a conference taking place in the no-longer-existing Reunion Arena in Dallas. I purchased a ticket as fast as humanly possible, and I counted down the days until I would see this man in person. He had changed my life—and he didn't even know who I was. I'll never forget my feeling of anticipation, sitting in my seat, waiting for my hero. Speaker after speaker took the stage until it was finally time for John C. Maxwell.

"Ladies and gentlemen, please welcome to the stage the world's number one authority on leadership, John Maxwell!"

Even as I'm writing about this experience, I have tears of joy and gratitude in my eyes. When John C. Maxwell himself calmly took the stage and slowly waved his hand to the sold-out arena, I had chills.

As he finished his speech, I again thought to myself, *I have to meet him someday!* And I wasn't thinking of a stalker or crazy-fan encounter. I wanted to thank him for using his God-given abilities to make this world a better place. I don't get starstruck very easily. I've met and done life with pretty much everyone I've ever wanted to meet. I've sat in the homes of the most famous people in the world, from Carrie Underwood to Shaquille O'Neal. I've conducted business with billionaires, and I've golfed with Pudge Rodríguez, Troy Aikman, and many other Hall of Fame athletes. I only mention that to say I'm not easily dazzled. I simply and truly wanted to tell John C. Maxwell thank you!

The Green Room

By my twenties, I had become a multimillionaire and was being asked to speak about how I accomplished that. One particular invitation was to an event at Reunion Arena, the same place I'd watched John C. Maxwell speak. As she always does to help me prep for a speaking engagement, my executive assistant emailed me the run of show: I like to know what's taking place before and after I speak so I can add as much value as possible. But this usual prep became highly unusual when I saw who was speaking right before me: John C. Maxwell! My first thought was *Whom did I so infuriate that I'm assigned to speak after John Maxwell!?* My second thought was *I'm going to meet John Maxwell!*

Before the day arrived, I prayed and thought about what I would say to my hero if I actually got to meet him. I thought the green room—

where refreshments, bathrooms, and makeup are available to speakers and where we get mic-ed up—might be the place. I knew what time John would be in the green room to get a mic on, and as I make my way to the arena, all I can think about is what I am going to say to him. (I literally worked more on that than on my ninety-minute speech!) John Maxwell had reached Stage 5, and he was the reason I had too. Without him, I don't know where I'd be. That's why I'm forever committed to preserving and expanding his legacy, and I pray that God will use me to impact someone the way He used John to impact my life.

The car pulls up to the arena and drops me off. I'm now backstage, headed to the green room—and to say I felt a *swarm* of butterflies would be a dramatic understatement. I hear the crowd in the sold-out arena… for just a second. Then I'm totally focused on the words I know God placed in my heart to tell John. I enter the green room, look to my left, and there he is, five feet away from me. I'm looking at John C. Maxwell.

Before I Could Say a Word…

"Logan, my friend! Great to see you!"

John Maxwell knew my name!

"John, God put it on my heart to carry on and expand your legacy. I'm sure you have a lot of fans, a lot of people pulling at you. On a small level, I can relate. Knowing how many people would love to talk with you, I am so grateful to have this opportunity. I want to thank you for… changing my life. When I was seventeen, I read *Developing the Leader Within You*, and since then I've read every book you've written—and I'll read every book you ever write. I love you and appreciate you. Thank you!"

With tears in his eyes, John said, "I love you, too, my friend! I pray for winners, and God brought me you. Why don't you and your wife join me in Pebble Beach for a week of golf?"

What!!! Me??? Are you kidding me??!!

I calmly asked John when he was planning to go. "Next week," he said.

I looked to my left at my assistant and then back at John. I must have done this three times before John turned to my assistant and said, "Logan can make next week work, right?"

I was completely booked that week... but a week after that conversation, John and I were playing golf in Pebble. Since that day, John and I have become close friends. Not an Easter or Christmas goes by when we don't text each other. We've vacationed together and ministered to people in Fiji, Guatemala, and other countries. He even endorsed this book—and he is very careful about whose books he endorses.

Paying It Forward

A man who completely changed my life, whom I once dreamed of merely meeting, is now a close friend I'm privileged to be doing life with. This kind of thing doesn't happen for people who have not reached Stage 5. It's my version of the law of attraction: We don't attract what we want in life; we attract who we are.

My journey of personal growth took me to the highest of heights, to levels I never anticipated years ago. In fact, my first book, *Stout Advice*, would have never happened if John C. Maxwell hadn't told me I should write a book. Likewise, this book would not exist if John hadn't told me I needed to write another book. He has inspired me to reach levels in life I never knew possible! His teachings have enabled me to both navigate the adversities in life and appreciate my successes.

Imagine the experiences that await you in Stage 5. Imagine if you could meet anyone, do anything, go anywhere in the world. This book was written to help you understand the 5 Stages up front and give you realistic expectations of what kind of growing you will have to do in order to reach your goals. As you learn about the attributes of grit in Section II, you'll be more able to focus on developing those traits, reaching your true potential, and enjoying the life of your dreams.

Remember, though, that Stage 5 is Success, not perfection. We will never reach perfection, but we can experience life-changing results that we can share with others. And that sharing is one way we move from success to significance.

To close this section of the book, I want to offer a quick reminder. As you go through life, you will have new beginnings, new ventures, new relationships, and more, and each will require your moving through the 5 Stages.

Enjoy the Honeymoon.

Power through the Adversity.

Enjoy the Progress.

Resist Management Mode.

Reach Success for yourself and enable others to do the same.

I'm beyond excited for you. I hope to hear your story and even meet you one day soon. And I can't wait to read *your* book(s) one day!

Logan and his good friend John Maxwell having
fun in Guatemala before a national conference.

SECTION II
ATTRIBUTES OF GRIT

Everything should be made as simple as possible, but no simpler.
—**Albert Einstein**

I'm convinced that simple is best. That's why I work to simplify my businesses, speeches, mentoring sessions, and even my sports programs. For example, to simplify baseball for my young Dallas Patriot athletes, I break down the game into its four basic components: pitching, fielding, hitting, and running the bases. If we win at each of these four components, we win the game. And what does this have to do with grit?

We have established that grit is the *bridge between where you are now* and *where you want to be.* In essence, grit is the vehicle that takes you *where you want to be.* Like any vehicle, grit has parts or *components.* Remove any one component, and it won't operate at its optimal level. Each component contributes to how well the vehicle runs. The same is true in baseball. Remove the component of good hitting, you lose. Remove good pitching, you lose. Remove good fielding… You get the idea.

So I have broken down grit into its simplest components, which I call *attributes.* Remove any one of these key attributes, and the vehicle simply won't perform at its best. Furthermore, a high Grit Factor—an efficiently running and finely tuned vehicle—requires all the components to be functioning well. And *well* means "well," not perfect—and don't aim for perfect. After all, rating a ten on the Grit Factor Scale is impossible.

Be aware, however, that a really low score on one attribute of grit lowers our scores on the other attributes. In fact, our scores for the attributes of grit we excel in will eventually drop because we overcompensate in order to make up for low-rated attributes. Do you see that this scoring system makes every attribute of the Grit Factor important? If we don't work on developing all the attributes of the Grit Factor, our scores on even our best-rated attributes will eventually drop lower and lower. The result will be fatigue, frustration, and eventually failure. You see, *we don't reach our bullseyes in life when we don't understand the need to develop all the attributes of grit.* Each and every one of the fifteen is essential to growing and sustaining the Grit Factor necessary to dominate in all endeavors.

Finally, now that you're at the heart of this book, you may find yourself thinking, *if only I'd had known this earlier in my journey, I wouldn't be where I am today.* Well, as motivational speaker and author Zig Ziglar said: "You don't have to be great to start, but you have to start if you're gonna be great!" And you *have* begun!

It's time to dive into developing your Grit Factor—and I'm excited for you! This book will grow you in ways you never expected if you will simply stay the course!

So I pray you will start immediately and soon find yourself devouring this book. I pray you'll read it cover to cover and then share it with people you love so they can grow with you. And I hope one day to meet you in person, high-five you, and congratulate you on the success you achieved because you increased your grit!

I also hope you will connect with me on social media so I can both follow your journey and encourage you along the way! My social media accounts can be accessed at www.LoganStout.com, where you'll also find my coaching, mentoring, and live-event information. Please connect with me and share your journey, testimonials, and more!

Chapter 7

SELF-DISCIPLINE

All success begins with self-discipline. It starts with you!
—Dwayne "The Rock" Johnson

T he word *discipline* originated from *discipulus*, the Latin word for *pupil.* That's why the Bible refers to Jesus' students as *disciples.* Then, in the 1300s, the word became associated with the military, and that's why, by the early 1500s, *discipline* came to mean "orderly conduct as a result of training." So today, when we see a skilled soldier, a star athlete, or even an obedient child, we say, "That person is well disciplined!"

Although I do admire a soldier's discipline, most soldiers don't become super achievers after their time in the military. Likewise, only a small percentage of well-disciplined athletes in college go on to sports careers after graduation, and then after they stop playing, they don't usually win any gold medals, figuratively speaking. Maybe a few well-disciplined children do become super achievers in adulthood. Yet some of these one-time well-disciplined individuals change. They relax, become less driven, and seem content to not achieve their full potential. Why?

I believe the reason is this: the three groups of people I've mentioned were disciplined at one point in their lives, but their discipline came from an outside force. An external factor held them accountable. They had been *extrinsically* motivated rather than *intrinsically* motivated. The commanding officer disciplined the soldier, the coach disciplined the athlete; and the parents disciplined their child. Once these external forces were removed from their lives, these individuals were without their driving force. Once they were doing life solo, they seemed to be missing a key characteristic of all super achieving individuals: self-discipline.

The First Victory

"In reading the lives of great men," said President Harry Truman, "I found that the first victory they won was over themselves... self-discipline with all of them came first." Great people, past and present, have developed the ability to win the battle within themselves. They have mastered self-discipline if not completely at least enough to do great things.

Let's consider how Webster's defines the word:

> *Self-discipline*: the ability to control one's feelings and overcome one's weaknesses; the ability to pursue what one thinks is right despite temptations to abandon it.

Wow! "The ability to pursue what one thinks is right despite temptations to abandon it"! That's a tall task! Yet President Truman recognized this as the *first* victory that must be won. Similarly, I've put self-discipline first on my list of the attributes of grit.

So—look again at Truman's quote—in the context of *The Grit Factor*, what is "right"? What should we be pursuing no matter what? I believe that what is right for you comes down to your bullseye exercises. You and I need to stay on track if we're to hit our bullseyes! To be very specific, then, self-discipline is our ability to pursue our bullseyes despite temptations to abandon them.

This kind of self-discipline requires an element of *focus*. We need to be able to block out distractions and temptations. In fact, focus makes the difference between good intentions and the effective actions. In baseball, self-discipline is key especially when it's your turn to hit. You see, most of the time the pitcher doesn't get the hitter out. The hitter actually gets himself out by swinging at a bad pitch or perhaps at the wrong pitch for the situation. For hitters, looking for the right pitch requires a lot of self-discipline. As they look for their pitch, they have to exercise self-discipline and not swing at everything the pitcher tempts them with.

Choosing Right Thoughts

Do you remember the process required to build a bridge from where you are to where you want to be?

Thoughts ➡ Actions ➡ Habits ➡ Results

Our thoughts lead us to act a certain way. Our actions can lead to habits. And habits lead to results. With the right habits, we get the right results. And the starting point for those right results is, yes, right thoughts.

Throughout the day, we could be thinking a whole lot of different thoughts. Self-discipline, though, is thinking only those thoughts that align with our bullseyes. Distractions will pop up—they always do. That's why we put around ourselves various reminders of our bullseyes. Whether we put a picture of our kids on our office desk or use lipstick to write our bullseyes on the bathroom mirror, we can set up our environment to help us discipline our thoughts and stay focused on our bullseyes.

Just as we have an infinite number of thoughts to choose from, we face an infinite number of possible actions at any specific moment in the day. But only a small, limited number of those actions will take us toward our bullseyes, and self-discipline is doing only those actions that align with our bullseyes. Put another way, self-discipline serves as a GPS for daily living. A lot of times, trust me, these are actions you don't especially feel like taking. These actions are very likely boring, not exciting; dull, not glamorous; and seemingly inconsequential, even pointless—and they may be worthless if they're not done *consistently*.

So why are you doing some of the things you do? Maybe your emotions were high when you made the commitment—but that was months ago. Now, when no one is watching and you've calmed down, will you still do what you said you would? At this point self-disciplined individuals—people with a high Grit Factor—separate themselves from everyone else. These self-disciplined individuals are victorious in the inner battle Harry Truman was talking about. This choice to persevere is the first victory you must win if you're ever going climb to the peak of Success Mountain!

In fact, by way of self-disciplined thoughts and actions, you will ultimately become a person of under-control habits, careful decisions, and extraordinary results. You'll be doing daily what most of the people around you wish they were doing and know they *should be* doing but aren't. You'll be climbing while they're still dreaming. You'll be in winning the game while they're still sitting on the bench.

Fuel for the Victory

When you choose to do the right things repeatedly over an extended period of time, you will win! Only self-discipline will fuel such consistency. Self-discipline makes the difference between short-term gains and long-term success, the difference between one-hit wonders and Hall of Fame icons. As I've warned you, self-discipline isn't typically fun and exciting; it's usually mundane and repetitive. But anything truly worth doing takes longer, costs more, and requires more self-discipline than you ever imagined—and that's how you know that what you're doing will be worth it!

Finally, as a society and as individuals in our society, we need to stop looking for shortcuts. Get rid of the lottery mind-set and embrace instead a self-disciplined mind-set. Stop asking, *how fast can we get there?* and start asking, *how far can we go?* With self-discipline, the journey has no limits. Without self-discipline you will hit dead end after dead end. The choice is yours.

Action Steps to Increase Your Grit Factor

- What is something you've started and stopped—maybe several times? Now, having read about self-discipline, what insights do you have as to why you stopped? Why might the results be different now?
- Who among your coworkers, neighbors, friends, fellow gym rats, and people at church comes to mind when you think of

self-discipline? Sit down and talk with that person about what he/she has done—and continues to do—to maintain that level of self-discipline.

- Having spent some time thinking about self-discipline, revisit your six bullseyes. Applying your new understanding and self-awareness, update the Downhill Habits. Then add to or fine-tune the Uphill Habits that will replace the Downhill and enable you to be more self-disciplined in all aspects of life.

Chapter 8

EXCELLENCE

We are what we repeatedly do. Excellence, then, is not an act, but a habit.

—Aristotle

One fruit of self-discipline is the desire to do things with excellence. In fact, excellence characterizes anyone and everyone who has a high Grit Factor. These individuals do everything with excellence—and Navy SEALs prove my point. These elite military officers are the ultimate example of grit. This brief look at SEAL training offers insight into how their Grit Factor is developed.

In a commencement speech he gave in 2014, Naval Admiral William H. McRaven—himself a SEAL—presented "10 Fundamental Life Lessons" he learned as a Navy SEAL. He calls them "little things that can change your life... and maybe the world." Imagine the audience's surprise when number one on the list was simply "Make your bed." At first glance, that seems unremarkable rather than at all inspiring. But let me share a few sentences from the admiral's speech, and you'll see how excellence is integral to SEAL training from the very moment cadets get out of bed. I've highlighted key words:

> *Every morning* in SEAL training, my instructors, who were all Vietnam veterans, would show up in my barracks room, and the *first* thing they'd do was inspect my bed. If you did it right, the corners would be square, the covers would be pulled tight, the pillow centered just under the headboard, and the extra blanket folded neatly at the foot of the rack. It was a *simple* task, mundane at best. But every morning we were required to make our bed to *perfection*... Making your bed will reinforce the fact that the *little things in life matter*. If you can't do the little things *right*, you'll never be able to do the big things *right*.

Notice two key words: *every morning*. Excellence isn't required of SEALs *sometimes*. Nor is it required only when they *feel like it*. Excellence is the standard *every morning*—and throughout every day. As basketball legend Michael Jordan put it, "Excellence isn't a one-week or one-year deal. It's a constant."

Excellence Always

Based on my own personal experience, I can tell you that this habit of excellence, this striving for perfection, is fundamental to the thinking of *all* superstar athletes and coaches. "Perfection is not attainable. But if we can chase perfection, we can catch excellence," said legendary football coach Vince Lombardi. Kobe Bryant shares that mind-set: "What I'm doing right now, I'm chasing perfection."

Motivational speaker Jim Rohn said, "If you care at all, you'll get some results. If you care enough, you'll get incredible results." I agree.

Quite frankly, if you're *not* doing something with *excellence*, I interpret that as you're *not* caring enough. I see it as a sign of apathy—and I am *not* a fan of apathy. Ask anyone I do life with "What upsets Logan the most?" Some will say, "Not doing something with excellence." Others might say, "Not doing my best." Same idea. They know I'm not a fan of apathy—of halfway efforts and low standards—and you shouldn't be either!

I'll never forget a team member (most companies use the word *employees*, but for me, the people who work with me are teammates) I had to fire because she had *Just Enough* Disease. Whatever was asked of her, she always did *just enough*. No matter how many times I coached her on this issue, she always had an excuse for her *just enough* performance. The final straw was when I asked her to find a potential incentive-trip location we could use for our top salespeople. I told her that I'd take my family, call it our vacation, and, at the same time, check out the spot for the company. Now, if you're my teammate and I tell you that I'm taking my family on this trip, wouldn't you realize this isn't just another trip? Long story short, the ex-teammate found very few options, all of them too expensive for the number of people we were looking at taking. I realized at that moment that she simply didn't understand this fundamental: excellence isn't an option; it's the rule. Ultimately, I found a better place at a better price on my own, and that was that.

Making It a Habit

Performing with excellence is the direct opposite of doing work apathetically. When I see the *habit of excellence* in people, I see that they are passionate about what they're doing, that they care about how well they're doing it, that they have a high Grit Factor, and that they are going to succeed. And if you're thinking, *I sure fall short here! I don't do everything in my day-to-day life with excellence*, know that I've been there!

At times I haven't had for myself a standard of excellence for the mental, physical, spiritual, financial, emotional, or relational aspects of my life. But I didn't stay there, so not to worry. Let me share with you what helped me develop my habit of doing things with excellence.

The tool is a simple question that I ask myself—in some form or another many times a day. Here it is:

What can I do to make [fill in the blank] even better?

What can I do to make [my memory] even better?

What can I do to make [my body] even healthier?

What can I do to make [my relationship with God] even more pervasive?

What can I do to make [my financial situation] even more God-honoring?

What can I do to make [my ability to express my emotions] even better?

What can I do to make [this relationship] even more a source of joy?

I hope you see from this list how helpful this question can be every day, throughout the day. Even at a recent leadership team meeting in a health-and-wellness company I own, someone came up with a great idea. I loved it; we all loved it. Yet I encouraged the group by asking, "How can we make this idea even better?" And we did.

In every aspect of your life, habitually asking yourself *How can I do [it] even better?* is a key to achieving excellence.

Action Steps to Increase Your Grit Factor

- Watch the YouTube video "2014 Texas Commencement Speech" by Admiral William H. McRaven. You might take notes and/or summarize the call to excellence you hear.

- Verbally affirm the excellence you see in the work habits of other people. Doing so will encourage their pursuit of excellence and perhaps inspire you as well.
- List daily tasks that you'd like to be more intentional about doing with excellence.
- List people in your life who seem to have made excellence a habit—and spend more time with them!
- Having done some thinking about excellence, revisit your six bullseyes. Applying your new understanding and self-awareness, update the Downhill Habits. Then add to or fine-tune the Uphill Habits that will replace the Downhill and enable you to achieve excellence in all aspects of life.

Chapter 9
PASSION

*If you don't love what you're doing with unbridled passion and
enthusiasm, you're not going to succeed when you hit obstacles.*
—Ralph Waldo Emerson

A s I mentioned in the previous chapter, excellence indicates
passion. People who are passionate about something tend to do
that something with excellence.

Many people *think* they are passionate. But consider Webster's
definition:

Passion: strong and barely controlled emotion.

In light of this definition, ask yourself, *"When was the last time I
felt so strongly about something that I could barely control my emotion"*?
Most people might have to look way back to their college days, or their

high school days, or as far back as their first crush. By my estimate, 95 percent of people today do not exhibit Webster's definition of *passio*n. Most people lack passion. Better put, most people are dead; they just haven't made it official yet! Somewhere along the way, they lost their zeal for life, and now they're living in a rut. And as someone has said, a rut is a coffin with the ends knocked out.

Early in the 2016 presidential race, Donald Trump faced off against sixteen opponents for the Republican nomination. One of his opponents was Jeb Bush. On paper, Jeb had the education and experience necessary for the job. He had the name recognition and a team of smart people behind him. And Jeb was the most well-funded of all seventeen candidates. But Jeb Bush lacked one crucial thing. He lacked *passion*. As soon as Donald Trump labeled him "Low-Energy Jeb," all hope for a Jeb Bush nomination went out like a light. Please don't take this as a reflection of my political views, but as an illustration of the importance of passion. Who wants to be around a low-energy person? Not me! Low-energy people lack passion. They're dull. They're boring. A brief aside. Don't confuse passion with noise or charisma. I know a lot of very quiet, introverted people who are hugely passionate about their work, their family, or a cause that matters to them.

Low-energy people aren't the only ones I have trouble being around. I'm sure you've known people you can't stand being around because, for instance, they're so negative! When you see them coming, you turn and run the other way. Why? Because negative people make us negative. The same thing can happen when we're around someone who always seems to worry. Suddenly, we start to worry! We too easily become like the people we choose to be around. That's why I often say, "Alignment before assignment!" The company we keep can mean the difference between a dream and a nightmare. And passionate people are rarely the cause of nightmares. If we want to succeed at any given task, we first need to align ourselves with positive, motivated, energetic, creative people.

They're Magnetic!

Passionate people attract people! Passionate people are *magnetic*! I once heard it put this way, "If you're on fire, people will come from miles to watch you burn!" It's true, and legendary basketball announcer Dick Vitale is my favorite example of this. I love what my good friend and Hall of Fame coach Del Harris says about Dick Vitale: "He's got the perfect face for radio." With his crooked nose, sagging eyelids, wrinkled face, and a head that's bald except for a few scraggly gray hairs, you would *not* expect this guy—of all people—to captivate millions on live TV, but he does! Why? Because Dick Vitale is passionate! Hands down, he is the most passionate announcer there is. Viewers *feel* his energy even through the screen. And because he's excited, he makes us excited. His passion for the game draws us in! Heck, no one really remembers what he says or why he says it, but watching basketball is simply better with him on the mic!

In sharp contrast to Dick Vitale, passionate people can also be idiots with horrible messages, yet sometimes we can't seem to turn the channel. I'm guessing you can think of people you simply don't agree with, but their passion captivates you, and you find yourself thinking, *I just gotta hear what they are going to say this time!* On the other hand, really big intellects who have a deep well of knowledge may struggle to get anyone to listen to them. It's just true: a passionate idiot will have a bigger audience than a brilliant intellect who lacks passion.

People with a high Grit Factor are definitely *passionate*. They *love* what they do. They speak with *enthusiasm*. They have a *zeal*, a *zest* for life. There is *vigor*. There is *emotion*. There is *fire!* To quote the great Yogi Berra, "Whatever you do, you should do it with feeling." That's right. Super achievers do things with feeling, with strong and sometimes barely controlled *emotion*. They do things with passion.

And I've always believed and taught that *passionate excellence beats miserable intelligence*. Passionate excellence is sportscaster Dick Vitale in the basketball world, Lee Corso in the football world, and Harry Caray in the baseball world. These three human magnets have drawn audiences around the world. They are real-life examples of passion's law of attraction.

Passionate About the *Why*

Back to Low-Energy Jeb. He didn't win his party's nomination; Donald J. Trump did. And, showing tremendous grit, Trump went on to win the presidential election. (Again, I'm not making a political statement here; I'm simply proving a point.) Hear President Trump's Grit Factor in his own words: "Without passion, you don't have energy. Without energy, you have nothing!" Regardless of political views, I believe we can all agree that President Trump can be described as passionate! Now, to be honest, you won't always be passionate about *what* you do, but you should always be passionate about *why* you do it. One of the most misleading statements I hear people make is "If you love what you do, you'll never work a day in your life." This is simply not true because we won't always love every aspect of what we need to do. But passionate, high-grit people push through. Here's the reality: If you love *why* you do *what* you do, you will be far more successful than those who don't have any… passion.

So, just as life is tough at times, work is hard at times. But nothing that's worthwhile will always be easy. You'll have days when the task is 100 percent work no matter how passionate you are about your profession. Heck, I hate being away from my family, and that can sometimes make me hate *what* I have to do. But I can't change the world from my couch! And I can't imagine *not* pursuing my *why*.

And my *why* is to add value to people's lives. To see people do life better. To help *everyone* understand that they are hardwired for success. But I can't do that without doing some things I don't want to do. I can't put one million people in my house and mentor them. I need to be active on social media. I need to travel to the audiences. I firmly believe—and I'm paraphrasing Les Brown—that *if you do today what others won't, you will have tomorrow what others don't.* Even when what you have to do isn't enjoyable, your *why* can keep you going. No matter how hard things got, my mom's *why* kept her grinding through—and her *why* was my brother and me! Her life was hard, and she made huge sacrifices for us. We were her passion! We were the fuel that kept her going.

What's your fuel? What's your why? You've just identified your passion! So be addicted to living! In everything be passionate, for each second is a blessing! We all have the ability to change the world for the better. Never take that gift for granted!

Passion and Purpose...

But what if you're not sure about your *why*? I'm often asked how a person can find passion. Here's a simple question to help you: What are you doing in those moments when you realize there's nowhere else you would rather be, those moments when you wish time could stand still? My list of such moments includes holding my kids, vacationing, spending time with my family, and being in the middle of the ocean. However, those wonderful moments don't pay the bills. Wouldn't it be great if they did?

Your *why* for whatever you do to earn a living is so you can do those I-wish-time-could-stand-still things. So, my work-related answer to this passion question is simple: When I have the honor of being a keynote speaker/trainer, there's nowhere else I'd rather be. I love making a difference for the companies that hire me and for the people who hear me. I'm truly in my sweet spot on stage. I'm also passionate when I'm coaching kids in baseball. I love it!

God has blessed me with great success in business as well as baseball, the two aspects of life about which I'm most passionate. And I hope you see from the examples I have shared the importance of clarifying your passion and your purpose—and understanding the difference. Your passions are what you absolutely *love* doing more than anything. Your talents are what you are *really* good at. And…:

The following truths will help you find your purpose and ultimately fulfill as much of your potential as possible:

1. You can be, do, and have more.
2. Pursuing your purpose will 100 percent require making sacrifices.
3. The sacrifice *is* worth it
4. The people you allow in your life will make or break you. They either keep you stuck or help you grow.
5. Reaching your potential is a process. It will take time, and it requires a plan.
6. Success rarely, if ever, happens without perseverance. Stick with your goal of fulfilling your potential!

And Talent

A lot of passionate people are horrible at what they're doing. I've seen people, for example, passionately sing without any talent whatsoever! Singing is clearly not their purpose in life. I've also seen extremely talented singers who have no passion for singing. Singing isn't their purpose in life either. Singers who are both passionate and talented are the ones we hear on the radio. Similarly, I'm extremely talented at both of my work-related passions: speaking and coaching. So, my talent plus my passion make both of those my purpose in life.

But how do you know if you're talented? Results! A story about a struggle I had years ago will offer an answer. I struggled with whether or not I should continue coaching baseball. As a baseball coach, I won nineteen world championship titles and a USA Baseball Championship gold medal. I also have one of the highest, if not *the* highest, winning percentages of any coach in history. My more than 1,400 victories have given me a career winning percentage of over 90 percent. Documentation beats conversation.

So I chose to stay on the track set forth in the Passion + Talent = Purpose equation. It kept me on point. And had I stopped coaching, I would have missed far too many amazing experiences, memories and life-changing moments. I don't say this to brag, but rather to make a very important point: a lot of *American Idol* rejects live on this planet. I don't mean that literally. What I mean is, a lot of people are trying to make a career out of something they are passionate about, but simply don't have the talent for. As a result, they move further and further away from their purpose in life.

On the long-running TV show and singing competition *American Idol*, contestants would go on stage and sing in hopes of ultimately earning a singing contract with a major label. From time to time, during the early auditions, you would see a competitor who absolutely could *not* sing. They were simply *terrible*! Knowing that Carrie Underwood got her big break on this show, I asked her about those singers. I thought their appearances were comedy bits to improve ratings—but they weren't! Carrie explained that those people really thought they could sing and actually believed they had a chance of winning. The truth is, sometimes people don't realize their talent—or lack thereof. (I wondered, *why didn't their friends keep them from embarrassing themselves on nationwide TV?*) When we are passionate about something but not talented, it's a *hobby*, not a purpose. We should not plan on earning a living doing this activity; that's what our free time is for.

Again, a purpose combines your passion and talent so you can make a career out of what you love doing. If you're great with people, you'll probably be talented at sales. Now find a product or service you are passionate about and—BAM!—you have a career based on your purpose. If you're talented at sales but not passionate about *what* you're selling or *why* you're selling it, you'll get burned out and feel empty inside no matter how much money you make.

Passion is essential to your Grit Factor. And you must have passion if you're going to know success!

Action Steps to Increase Your Grit Factor

- Name three to five people in your life who live with great passion. What can you do to increase your time with one or more of them?
- Consider your eating habits and even do some research. What food and drinks are you consuming that lower your energy levels? What should you be consuming *less* of? What should you be consuming *more* of? It's difficult to be passionate when our diets are making us lethargic.
- Join a social group, a networking group, or any other group that enables you to associate with passionate people.
- Join a gym. Your body carries your mind. Exercise addresses the physical component of being consistently passionate and

energized. You are always just one workout away from being in a great mood!

- What are your passions? What are your talents? What, then, is your purpose in life?
- Having spent some time thinking about passion, revisit your six bullseyes. Applying your new understanding and self-awareness, update the Downhill Habits. Then add to or fine-tune the Uphill Habits that will replace the Downhill and enable you to be more passionate in all aspects of life.

Chapter 10

VISION

Vision is the art of seeing things invisible.
—**Jonathan Swift**

I n the world of motivational speaking and writing, *vision* is in vogue. Communicators talk about *visionaries* and cite examples like Steve Jobs and Walt Disney. Yet the idea seems somewhat mysterious and the possibility of actually ever having a vision for one's life, unreachable for mere mortals. We infer that only the greatest minds among us are able to have a vision—but nothing is further from the truth. In fact, I believe one of the unique gifts that our Creator has given us humans is the gift of *vision*.

Let me make it simple by giving you my definition:

Vision: *seeing what others don't.*

That's what it is. When you "see" what others don't, you are—by definition—a visionary.

Consider what Robert F. Kennedy said: "Some men see things as they are and ask why. I dream things that never were and ask why not." Clearly, Kennedy was a person with *vision*. But perhaps one of the best examples of a person of *vision* was Leonardo da Vinci. This artist, sculptor, and painter was also the first to *see* flying machines and parachutes. His journals are actually full of ideas that were way before his time.

Sapere Vedere

We all know that seeing is believing. In fact, you might be the one who always says, "Show me!" and there is great value in actually seeing something with our own eyes. But this insistence to see reveals a lack of vision. Remember doubting Thomas, the apostle in the Bible who refused to believe that Christ had risen from the dead? Thomas declared that he would not believe until he had seen Christ and actually touched his wounds. Being a doubting Thomas has its limitations—and doubting Thomas types aren't usually very successful.

Now consider being more of a Leonardo di Vinci who summed up his philosophy for life in these two words: *sapere vedere*, Latin for "learning to see beyond the clouds." A more specific definition breaks down the two words: *sapere* ("knowing how") and *vedere* ("to see"). *Sapere vedere* is "knowing how to see." Da Vinci did not believe that seeing is believing; his philosophy was believing is seeing. When all the world was seeing the clouds, da Vinci chose to look beyond the clouds. He saw what could be, not merely what is.

To that point, I believe that being a person of vision is a conscious decision we must make on a daily basis. That's why one of my prayers every morning is this: *God, grant me the wisdom, the clarity, and the vision that surpasses all understanding.* Read that again. Consider making that your own prayer. Simply put, I'm asking God to grant me vision, to give me the ability to see what others don't.

Some Practical Examples

In business, I've always believed that the secret to making a lot of money is seeing a big problem before it happens and solving it before anyone else does. This approach requires vision. In sports, I believe one key to my success as a coach is vision. I am able to see my athletes not only as they are, but also as what they can become! In fact, I apply that very principle as I coach: I ask my players to mentally see themselves hitting the ball before they go up to bat. I believe we see success in our minds before we make it happen. I'm 100 percent confident these vision exercises I do with my players, even the subtle ones they don't know we're doing, contribute to my coaching success. I call this method "transfer of belief" and "transfer of vision." (I love to take this training to corporations. So many light-bulb moments!)

So, for example, I say, "I can't wait to see you hit his curveball" to a player who has struggled with this. Then I ask, "Where are you going to hit it?" When I know for certain that he believes he's going to hit it and that he's clearly imagined himself doing so, I walk away. More often than not, the player gets the hit. Why? Because he envisioned himself hitting that curveball. I had transferred my belief *in* him… *to* him. Now he believes he can hit curveballs.

I use transfer of belief with my sons all the time. I affirm them with, "How cool is it going to be when you can dress yourself and don't need Mommy and Daddy's help?!" Sure enough, a few minutes later Miles and Cooper will come walking into my bedroom all dressed. "We did it, Dad! We dressed ourselves!"

Many people don't know this, but I'm also a professional scout for Major League Baseball. Even in this line of work, I attribute my success to my vision. Other scouts tend to focus on a prospect's weakness and say things like, "He's too slow. What position will he play?" or "He'll never make it at the next level!" But I focus on the prospect's strengths, saying to myself, *Yeah, but who cares that he's slow? He just hit the ball five hundred feet!* And that's a real-life example. Chris Davis, one of my former players, finally did get drafted. He's had his ups and downs as all players do, but he also had one of the most successful MLB seasons in history. He's been an All-Star, led MLB in homers, and more. He's accomplished what most kids only dream of, but other scouts downplayed his abilities. In my opinion, those scouts were visionless.

Having vision helps us in so many aspects of life.

Seeing Possibility as Reality

There are no traffic jams near the top of Success Mountain. Most people—and I'm talking 95 percent—stay stuck at the base. Their vision—or *lack* of real vision—has them seeing all the reasons why *not* to climb: the dangerous cliffs, the jagged rocks, the blowing wind, and the tough conditions. They see the clouds—these realities—as reasons why they shouldn't even try to get to the top. That's why most people never fulfill their potential.

Strengthening their resolve to not even try to ascend Success Mountain is the company they're keeping at the base. These people are reinforcing for each other the validity of their reasons—excuses—not to try. They all stay together, thinking the same thoughts and often throwing community pity parties. Misery loves company—and they've made misery their *comfort zone.*

Successful people, however—those individuals who have a high Grit Factor—see the possible benefits and blessings of climbing Success Mountain. They realize, for instance, that there's more to life than what they're currently doing. They know something is missing, and they can't wait to figure out what it is. They decide to start their journey, and suddenly they have a new vision for their life. They see in their mind what life could be like once they reach the top! Even before they get there, they feel the excitement and thrill of having made it to the summit! Obstacles? Cliffs? Dangers? What dangers? They don't *see* the dangers. They live with the mind-set of Henry Ford, who said, "Obstacles are those frightful things you see when you take your eyes off your goal." Once these people reach the top, they experience a bit of déjà vu. You see, they've been at the summit before... in their mind's eye!

Based on my own personal experience, I know vision is a great separator between the haves and the have-nots. Each single one of the all-star athletes, millionaires, and billionaires I've met has vision. There are no exceptions! Vision is a key component of their Grit Factor. These individuals *see* what others don't. In real estate, they are the agents who see the property as it can be. In business, they are the entrepreneurs who see potential while others just see problems. As leaders of people, these men and women of vision see others (teammates, employees, business partners, customers, and clients) as they can be. And—far more importantly—when these people look in the mirror, they see themselves as they can become, which reminds me of the famous picture of the cat looking in the mirror and seeing a lion!

Vision Boards

By now I hope you're thinking, *Okay, Logan, so how can I become a person of vision, a person who sees beyond the clouds?* This is definitely the question you should be asking—and I'm glad to answer it. But first realize this: We don't see things as *they* are; we see them as *we* are. That's right. It's back to you and your development of yourself! As you yourself grow, your ability to see the potential in others—and even in yourself— will grow. In other words, as you yourself grow, your vision grows!

In the King James Bible, Proverbs 29:18 says, "Where there is no vision, the people perish." To achieve success, you must have vision for your destination. With no vision, you'll have no reason to push ahead because, without vision, you have no place to go.

As you move in the direction of your visions, I assure you they will grow. I remember, for instance, when my vision was to earn six figures a year. As I got closer to that, my vision grew to earning a million dollars a year. Then suddenly my vision was to earn a million dollars a month, and eventually my vision grew to earning a million dollars a day. It took the smaller initial vision to lead me to today's vision: give away $1 million a week to my church and the causes I care the most about.

Though some of us are more visual than others, all of us can answer these questions to one degree or another:

What visions are occupying valuable space in my mind?
When I think of my job, what do I see?
When I think of my marriage—or lack thereof—what do I see?
When I think of my body, what do I see?

The list can go on, but I'm sure you got the pattern.

Also, remember that vision isn't simply *how* you see yourself; it's also *where* you see yourself. Whatever your visions are, that's where you're headed! And we're going to get those right visions right now! Go back to your six bullseyes, and for each aspect of life, you're going to make a vision board. This may sound corny to some of you, but I assure you it's worthwhile.

Vision Boards

First, your vision board *must* be something you see *every* day. It can be something you create and use as your screen saver for your phone and computers. Or maybe it goes on your bathroom mirror, so you see it every morning and night.

Here are some examples of what I have on my vision board:

• **Emotional**: Patience is not my best quality, yet I still need to treat people with love, compassion, and grace. The better I am emotionally, the better everything around me will be. My family, teams, and supporters are all counting on me to be the most emotionally healthy leader possible so that I am able to handle well all that comes my way.

Youth Athletes Foundation (YAF) hosted the first annual Dallas Patriots Alumni game at Frisco's Rough Riders stadium. Shown here are current and past DP players at the event. (2018)

- **Relational**: This reminds me to spend my best time, not simply my leftover time, with the people I love the most. It's too easy to only have leftover time for the important people we're working to provide for. But being the best husband, dad, and friend takes some sacrificing and work.

Logan, Haley and the boys at Christmas. (2019)

- **Physical**: This pic of me playing beach volleyball reminds me of what I'm capable of. Remember, don't compare yourself to other people. It's OK to have people on your vision board you look up to, but don't idolize people or have unrealistic expectations for yourself based on someone else's abilities. You are perfect just the way you are! Well, when I lose these pesky ten pounds I will be. Ha!

When we look better, we feel better. Everyone desires to be their best self and that takes daily dedication. Stay in shape so you can participate in the world with confidence!

- **Spiritual**: I am not a religious person in the way many people think of "religious." I am a Christian, and I'll share what that means to me. I try to live according to the two most important lessons Jesus taught—love God and love people… I want to be *in* the world but not *of* the world. A saltwater fish lives its entire life in salt and won't survive outside of it. But when you catch a saltwater fish and cook it, you don't taste any salt. It's *in* the ocean, but not *of* the ocean… My passion is reaching people who don't yet follow God, people who have strayed, and people who are turned off by, or are struggling with, God, the church, and more… I want to love people, not judge people; connect with people, not correct people. Although some of my friends have different spiritual beliefs, I love them and they love me— and that's how it should be!

This picture reminds me of God's grace, love, and mercy. (I don't know where I'd be without him!) In Guatemala, John Maxwell had just spoken to thousands of soldiers, educators, and businesspeople—and more than eight thousand people accepted Christ as their Savior that day! I joined others in handing out more than eight thousand Bibles!

John had spoken on transformational leadership, and then he shared a ten-minute message about four pictures of God. Seeing the crowd's response was one of the most beautiful moments of my life. It reminds me that even people who are off track want to believe in God; they want the love of Christ. I want to reach those people. If they knew the God I know, they would run into his arms. He loves us and wants only the best for us.

*Transformational Leadership in Guatemala where
Logan and John C. Maxwell were keynote speakers.*

- **Financial**: I strongly desire to continue to both create wealth and help others do the same. I can't give what I don't have. Yes, I like nice things as well. (Nothing wrong with that!) I love entertaining people and have had the privilege to mentor on a yacht in the middle of the ocean! This pic is of the Youth Athletes Foundation, the nonprofit my wife and I started for kids in need. The more money we make, the more kids we can help. Side note: We have annual golf tournaments, a gala, and more, and I'd love to meet you at one of those events.

*Logan and Haley surprised their staff with a
private yacht excursion in the Bahamas. (2017)*

*Logan and John Maxwell arriving back in the USA from a week of
travel abroad sharing messages of encouragement and personal growth
around the world.*

The foundation started by Haley and Logan, Youth Athletes Foundation, hosts an annual golf tournament in Texas to raise money for kids to eliminate cost from preventing participation.

My vision board fuels the fire in my soul every time I see it! Your vision board should do the same for you. Make putting it together a priority—and make the time to do it right. Then, as you grow and accomplish more, keep updating your vision board.

My vision board keeps me dreaming. It keeps me from being complacent. It literally gives me images of why I do what I do every day. It also reminds me of why I avoid certain people, places, and things that distract me from working toward my goals.

Again, *vision* is the ability to see what others don't. God gave you visions for your life that only you can make happen. Your six bullseyes can serve as vision boards that you visit every day. Add the kind of vision board I just told you about to those six bullseyes and watch your visions become reality.

Action Steps to Increase Your Grit Factor

- What is your vision for your life? If you could design your life, what would it look like? Take time now to design your life. Create a vision for yourself and for those you care about.
- Make your vision board!
- When speaking to others, use your words to paint pictures of their better future. You could, for example, tell your daughter, "I see you one day performing on a big stage! The crowd will be huge, and they'll all be calling your name! You'll have to look out in the crowd for your two old parents. It'll be tough to spot us because of all the people, but of course we'll be there! I can just see it now!" Use those key words *I can see.*
- Having spent some time thinking about vision, revisit your six bullseyes. Applying your new understanding and self-awareness, update the Downhill Habits. Then add to or fine-tune the Uphill Habits that will replace the Downhill and enable you to become a person of clearer and even greater vision.

Chapter 11
OWNERSHIP

The price of greatness is responsibility.
—**Winston Churchill**

T
he ancient Greek writer Sophocles said, "It is a painful thing to look at your own trouble and know that you yourself and no one else has made it." That very contemporary sounding observation still rings true two thousand-plus years later. We human beings don't like to take responsibility for problems we brought on ourselves. Rather than look in the mirror, we tend to look for every—and any—other possible reason why things didn't work out the way we wanted. We blame other people, politics, the environment, our upbringing, our past—we can get pretty creative. Simply put, though, we position ourselves as the victim. As playwright George Bernard Shaw pointed out, "Liberty means responsibility. That is why most men dread it."

Your thoughts? I'm guessing you're either on board with what I'm saying, or a little voice in the back of your head is whispering your disagreement. *Yeah, but…* it says. *Yeah, but you don't know my situation.* Or *Yeah, but you don't understand my boss.* Or *Yeah, but you don't know what it's like!* Yeah, but *what?* Excuses don't cut it! "How could such-and-such be my fault?" you ask. Simple—and I'll let Roman emperor and philosopher Marcus Aurelius answer: "Our life is what our thoughts make it."

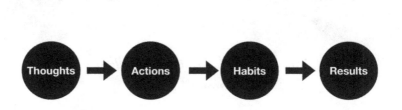

That's the formula. Our results—our life experience—begins with our thoughts. And who controls your thoughts? You do! Each one of us owns our thoughts. I like how Jim Rohn phrases this idea:

> The same winds blow on us all: the winds of disaster, opportunity, and change. Therefore, it's not the blowing of the wind, but the setting of the sail that determines our direction in life.

With our thoughts, each of us sets our own sail. Put another way, although we can't control what happens to us or around us, we can control how we think about and how we respond to all things in life. By choosing to *own* our thoughts, we choose to take control of our life and simply do life better.

The Other Option

The opposite of an *ownership* mind-set is a *victim* mind-set. When things go well, virtually everyone displays the ownership mind-set. "Self-made millionaire!" they claim. But what about when things go badly? I've never heard of a self-made bum! After all, when things go badly, people blame others.

When things go badly, 99 percent of the population plays the victim, revealing the victim mind-set they'd been hiding all along. *The economy is tough... No one wants to buy... People are skeptical... No one appreciates me...* On and on and on. I call this the Momentum Phenomenon. When things are going our way, we tend to think we are a lot better than we actually are. It's like an athlete playing over his head or having a hot streak. On the flipside, one's true colors come out when things are going badly. Panic mode typically sets in, and people either think they're more of a loser than they actually are, or they play the victim. They choose anything except taking full responsibility, which is the emotionally tough option. You see, I believe when people play the victim, they're trying to protect themselves from the emotional pain of facing the facts that they themselves are *weak,* and their words, actions, or decisions were *bad!* Listen, I understand that some excuses are 100 percent valid, but that doesn't resolve or change anything. We must *own* our thoughts, actions, habits, and results. Excuses prevent us from doing so.

Youth sports offers many opportunities for athletes to choose a victim mind-set and excuses. I'm still proud of an athlete who didn't make that choice. In 2016 I was coaching a Dallas Patriots baseball team. Mind you, I had no kid on the team, so I wasn't at all invested in who played and who didn't. All I wanted to do was mentor each kid to be his very best both on and off the field—and of course win whatever World Series we were playing.

Quick background to put this situation in context: The Dallas Patriots play at the highest level of baseball in the world for players ages 5u-18u. Every player who has gone through our program since 1999 has been given the opportunity to play college baseball, and a lot of guys who've gone through the Dallas Patriots now play professional baseball. Among our alumni are Trevor Story, Josh Bell, and Chris Davis, and there are a lot more. Every player has to try out for the Patriots, and all playing time is earned. The contract clearly states that no amount of playing time is guaranteed, but of course we would never take a player without fully expecting him to get plenty of playing time. Families come to the Dallas Patriots for the highest level of baseball coaching and mentoring. As I stated earlier, I personally have won a lot, served as a Major League scout since 2002, played pro baseball, coached college baseball, etc. Bottom line: I know what I'm doing. Okay, rant over! It's just that this story I'm about to tell you always gets me fired up. I cannot stand the victim mind-set. Drives me crazy!

We had just finished an incredible comeback victory in the last inning to win a big game. Unfortunately, one of our players had had the worst game of his career, and I pulled him from the lineup after he made three errors that nearly cost us the game. The player who stepped in actually got the game-winning hit and then made a diving catch to win the game for us. I had a great conversation with the young man I pulled out of the game, and he agreed he needed to be pulled. His exact statement to me was "Coach, I have zero confidence right now. I'm killing the team." After the game, he and I talked some more, and his spirits were good. We set a time to meet outside of regular team practices so we could fix his fielding mechanics and get his mind-set right. He owned the situation. His parents, however, were a different story!

Mic-Drop Moment

Mom and Dad were waiting for me in the parking lot. As soon as I saw them, I knew they wanted to discuss their son's playing time. I also noticed that their seventeen-year-old son wasn't standing with them. He was in the car. Clearly, he wasn't in agreement with whatever his parents were about to say. The parents were respectful, but simply delusional. They played the victim: "How could you pull our son from the game? What did he do to deserve this?" The questions kept coming until I finally couldn't take it anymore.

"Why don't you ask your son to step out of the car and let him answer your questions?" I said.

They agreed, and the magic happened. Their son said, "Mom and Dad, I agree with what Coach Stout did. I wasn't playing well, it wasn't going to get better during the game, and Coach saved me from costing the team the game. I own the results. They were no one's fault but my own, and tomorrow Coach and I are getting on the field to get my confidence back."

And, yes, if I'd had a mic, I would have dropped it. Turn out the lights on the pity party, send the crybabies home, and let's move forward. The player had an ownership mind-set. The parents, who had never played baseball in their lives, played the victims.

Unfortunately, most people are never taught the ownership mind-set. They live and embrace the victim mind-set. It becomes their story, and they live a life of unfulfilled potential. If you've lived your life blaming others, I want to help you snap out of it and take back the reins! Your life story isn't going to be a fairytale. It will be a biography that, like every biography, will have ups and downs in every aspect of life. Your response to the challenges and the tragedies will determine whether or not your bio has a heroic ending.

A Key Takeaway: Accountability

Let me introduce you to a simple equation that I hope you'll carry with you the rest of your life:

Many people talk about *attitude*. And many talk about *action*. Both are necessary. But few of us ever talk about *accountability*. For many, that's the piece missing from their achievement puzzle.

So, when you ask me, "Logan, what can I do to adopt an ownership mind-set?" I have two answers.

First, let yourself be held accountable. "Accountability breeds responsibility," said Stephen R. Covey, author of *The 7 Habits of Highly Effective People*. When we become *accountable*, we become *responsible*. When you are accountable to your boss for how you use your time, you become more responsible with your time. When you are accountable to your spouse for how you spend your money, you become more responsible with your money.

Whenever I speak to entrepreneurs, solopreneurs, business and sales teams, athletes and coaches, real estate agents, or whomever, I encourage every person to find an accountability partner or, even better, a coach. I believe, for instance, that most small-business owners fail because no one holds them accountable for their time, for their activity (or lack thereof), or for their results. An accountability partner fixes that because—as world-renowned motivational speaker Les Brown put it—"You can't see the picture when you're in the frame."

We all need someone observing us, giving us feedback, and holding us accountable. I have one-on-one coaching/mentoring clients as well as Hot Tables (groups of people with similar goals whom I coach/mentor) from all over the world. Why do they pay me to coach them? For the same reason athletes have personal coaches for what they do. All baseball players and golfers have a swing coach. Runners have a coach. Swimmers have a coach. In addition to saving us time and money, a personal coach leads us to our bullseyes with a lot less stress, not as much wasted time, and fewer squandered resources. Of all the various ways other people can help us succeed, holding us accountable may be the most effective.

A Key Takeaway: Own Your Thoughts

In addition to encouraging the acquisition of an accountability partner when someone asks me, "What can I do to adopt an ownership mind-set?" I also advise them to *own their thoughts*. Owning our thoughts is essential to the ownership mind-set and being accountable is essential to owning your thoughts. Accepting the reality that we are imperfect people who need the support that accountability provides will help us take control of our own thoughts. Accountability is key to you being able to stop letting others hijack your mind. Turn off Facebook. Turn off Twitter. Turn off the cell phone alerts that interrupt your focus. Turn off the TV. Turn off sports radio.

Do I use social media? Yes! I *use* it—but I don't get *used* by it. Do I watch TV? Yes, but the TV gets what's *left* of my day, not the *best* of my day! And let me tell you, when I was first building my businesses I cut out all that garbage. I went years without TV. I sacrificed. I stopped playing recreational sports at night. I missed a lot of family events. I sacrificed for my family and turning off the media was one of those sacrifices. We're all going to have to sacrifice at some point. Either you sacrifice now and play the rest of your life, or you spend the rest of your life having to sacrifice.

But back to owning your thoughts, let me get specific. Develop a daily personal-growth plan. Every day since I was seventeen, I've spent time on me first thing in the morning, and I don't know where I'd be without this habit. The greatest investment you will ever make is in yourself. So spend some quiet time in the morning to get your mind right. After all, you either make your way in the world, or it makes its way in you. In addition, too many people go through life with expired thoughts. Restock your mind each morning with fresh inventory.

Many of you are probably still wondering what a personal-growth plan looks like. It's *not* simply reading a positive self-help book. That's a personal-growth activity, but it's not a plan. Some good personal-growth plans are out there, but—call me biased—the Stout Mentoring personal-growth plan is what I recommend to everyone. It's the systematic approach I use to grow myself—and thousands of others. I've seen people follow this plan and take their mental, emotional, personal, relational, spiritual, and financial lives to levels they'd never imagined. If you would like to learn more about my mentoring program which has helped thousands of people, probably just like you, email info@LoganStout.com. Quite frankly, you cannot afford to *not* have a personal-growth plan if you truly want success. Also, be sure to read your bullseyes every morning so they can be like a GPS guiding you every step of each day.

Never Stop Dreaming!

Your personal growth plan and your bullseyes are essential to owning your thoughts because they will help you realize when negativity is trying to sabotage your day. Usually that negativity comes in the form of a person. It's undoubtedly happened to you. You see the phone number appear on the screen of your cellphone, you don't want to deal with this negative person, and even if you don't accept the call, your mood instantly goes downhill. Run from those people! Seriously! Avoid negative people. Avoid negative places. Go to the positive places where positive people are! Negativity paralyzes possibility!

Back in the early 1900s, before he was the wealthiest man on the planet and he had no money, Aristotle Onassis would seek out the restaurants that sold the most expensive coffee. Although he couldn't afford to eat at those places, he wanted to put his mind around things and people of abundance. He guarded his mind by being intentional about his environment. His actions may seem silly and worldly, but they worked to keep his eyes on his goal. His approach can work for you too. It works for me.

When I first got started in business ownership, I had my ups and downs, my self-doubt, and my pity parties, just like anyone else. When adversity hit, I used to sneak into a gated community so I could drive down the nicest street. There I saw the kind of home I wanted to provide for my family one day. I was twenty-one years old. That street—Monterey Drive in Frisco, Texas—was actually a part of my vision board. I remember parking and walking up and down Monterey Drive, thinking, *one day I'm going to live on this street!* I didn't know how I'd ever earn the money to do so, but I never stopped dreaming.

And at the age of twenty-seven, I bought my dream home on Monterey Drive. We had so much fun in that house! We had nine-piece bands perform private charity events for hundreds of people at a time! Yes, hundreds of people fit in our foyer! We housed nine kids who needed a place to stay, and we served them, fed them, mentored them, and loved them. We have so many amazing memories from our time in that home. Then the day came when it was time to upgrade. We wanted a more private community, where kids like me couldn't sneak in and walk up and down the street. Yes, my dream—and our home—got an upgrade!

When we work toward our dreams on a daily basis and we stay positive as we do so, we not only hit our bullseyes, but we imagine even better ones. Monterey Drive was a positive in my early years as an entrepreneur and thinking about one day having a home on that street kept me in a positive mind-set no matter how sideways things went. We need to stay focused on the possibilities, not the negatives.

Talking to Yourself

And our focus on possibilities involves self-talk. How do you talk to yourself? Are you constantly focusing on the negative? Be aware and be careful because thoughts shape our words and our actions. Are you telling yourself why something won't work? Are you constantly beating yourself up? Or are you building yourself up? Are you speaking life and positivity? You need to be able to answer these questions because *your attitude determines your altitude.*

In the past, every time I fell into negative self-talk or found myself thinking negative thoughts, I stopped by Monterey Drive. Today, I look at a picture of my boys. They are my new Monterey Drive! They also remind me that everything we do and say will impact someone in some way. I know my children watch everything I do and say. I want to leave them—and everyone I meet or mentor—better than they were when I found them.

And that goal is a matter of personal development. You must grow you. When you grow, everything around you grows. As you grow yourself, your self-talk will improve. You'll stop beating yourself up, and you'll start to realize all that you can do… no matter what life is trying to do to you.

Action Steps to Increase Your Grit Factor

- Pay attention to your self-talk. When you hear yourself saying, "The computer won't let me log on," you're thinking like a victim. When you realize that you can't log on and hear yourself saying, "I'll figure it out," you are thinking with an ownership mind-set. Work on eliminating the first kind of self-talk and increasing the second.

- On a scale from 1-10 (1 is the least, 10 is the most), rate the degree to which you have an ownership mind-set. Write down the number... Then write down any areas in your life where you tend to blame others. Do you need to adjust your rating?... Then ask five people—whom you can trust to be completely honest—to rate the degree to which you have an ownership mind-set. Tell them that they can't offend you... Next, with their input and your self-evaluation in mind, consider what you learned. And, if you feel ready, decide today that you will take full responsibility for every aspect of your life. Journal this proclamation.

- Find an accountability partner or, even better, a coach! If inclined, apply for personal coaching at LoganStout.com. Also, develop a personal-growth plan.

- Beware your associations! Don't spend a lot of time with victims! That mind-set too easily spreads!

- Unplug! Turn off the TV. Turn off Facebook. Turn off Twitter. In a word, control social media; don't let it control you.

- Having spent some time thinking about ownership, revisit your six bullseyes. Applying your new understanding and self-awareness, update the Downhill Habits. Then add to or fine-tune the Uphill Habits that will replace the Downhill and enable you to willingly take more responsibility for what you say and do in all aspects of life.

Chapter 12
SELFLESSNESS

In humility, be moved to treat one another as more important than yourself.

—Philippians 2:3 (NET Bible)

P
retty much everyone knows the name Troy Aikman, the three-time Super Bowl champ, six-time Pro-Bowl player, first-ballot Hall of Famer, and one of the greatest to ever play the game of football. I have the honor of knowing him on a personal level.

The final touches were being put on a new facility for one of my companies, and our *6 Core Values* had just been mounted onto the freshly painted walls of the front lobby. I remember discussing those *6 Core Values* with Troy, and I'd like to share those with you.

Troy Aikman and Logan entering Logan's office at IDLife Corporate Headquarters in Frisco, Texas. On display are the IDLIfe Core Values: People First, Freedom, Excellence, Ownership, Passion and Vision.

Our 6 Core Values

1. **People First**: Honor and respect every individual. Always make decisions based on what's right for people. Take care of your people, and everything else falls into place.

2. **Freedom**: Allow people freedom of thought, ideas, and creativity. Do what you can to help everyone accomplish their dreams, goals, and aspirations.

3. **Excellence**: Doing the right things *with excellence* leads to success. Strive for excellence in thoughts, actions, habits, and results.

4. **Ownership**: Own your life! Take responsibility for your thoughts, actions, habits, and results.

5. **Passion**: Be addicted to living! Be passionate in all you do. Remember that each second is a blessing! We all have the ability to change the world for the better. Never take this gift for granted!

6. **Vision**: See what others don't. Have a bullseye inside the bullseye. Let thoughts become things: see the future you want! Don't just *play* the game; *change* the game!

And in this chapter we're going to focus on *People First* because that principle for life—also called selflessness—is a component of grit.

People First, Team First

Troy is an embodiment of *People First*. He lives this core value daily, always giving and never asking for or expecting anything in return. His generosity in the public spotlight pales in comparison to the time and effort he gives behind the scenes on a daily basis. His establishment of the Troy Aikman Foundation (www.Aikman.com) further manifests Troy's desire to help others.

Notice that *People First* is number one on the list of *Our 6 Core Values*. Putting other people's needs and desires before your own is extremely countercultural in our narcissistic world of selfies and entitlement. Selfie-sticks! Are you kidding me? Ten years ago we all would have laughed at the idea a selfie. Now, I can't be too harsh because I, too, am guilty of taking an occasional selfie, and I take selfies with those of you who come to my events. I do want to say loudly, though, *be careful of the ego trap*!

It's human nature (is that an excuse?), but so many people think only of themselves. When I'm out in public and catch bits and pieces of the conversations around me, the topic is usually *me, me, and... more about me!* Virtually everyone is putting themselves first verbally and nonverbally too. To prove that second point, consider how most people judge a group photo. We *first* look at *ourselves* in the photo, don't we? If *I* look good, "Hey, this is a great photo!" It doesn't matter that everyone else's eyes are closed! Who cares? *I* look good, so it's a *good* picture!

That's a silly example, but it makes the point: individuals with a high Grit Factor put other people *first*. In sports, the *People First* mindset translates to a *team-first* attitude. As many people have heard me say countless times, individuals play the game, but teams win championships! In baseball, the home-run hitter lays down a sacrifice bunt to move the winning run to scoring position. In football, the lineman does his job to block the edges so the running back can sprint into the end zone.

You see the importance of *People First* teamwork in relationships as well. A husband and wife prioritize the other's needs ahead of his or her own. Where selfishness exists, the marriage will suffer! In parenting, *People First* is clearing your calendar to drive your kids halfway around the world for soccer practice!

The Best Role Models

The greatest leader of all time—Jesus of Nazareth—stated in no uncertain terms that he came to serve, not be served. (If you're not of the Christian faith, you can still learn some things here. Also, I have very close friends who aren't Christians. I love them, and they love me.) When I say, "the greatest leader of all time," I'm basing that on a metric we all can hopefully agree on number of followers. Jesus has more followers than anyone in history despite being in his leadership role for only thirty-three years. (Let that sink in for a second!) And Jesus was the very first to present humility as a leadership quality. In the Bible, *People First* is demonstrated by John the Baptist who said, "[Jesus] must become greater and greater, and I must become less and less" (John 3:30 NIV). Later, Paul said, "Let no one seek his own good, but the good of his neighbor" (1 Corinthians 10:24 ESV).

Now, if you don't believe in the Bible at all, let's look to the military for an example of *People First*. Can you imagine if the great men and great women of our military embraced a *me-first* attitude? The entire military establishment would collapse like a house of cards! Rather, the military exists and is effective only because of a *People First* mindset. Soldiers put their country first, and their country is, by definition, other people.

In the movies, we all admire the hero who dies for his family, the Secret Service agent who takes a bullet for his president, and the pilot who saves the lives of her passengers and crew but lost her own. In real life, we love the firefighter who runs into the burning building to rescue people; the police officer who risks being shot to protect the innocent, and the organ donor who gives a kidney to a sick patient. Whether you've seen it in the movies or experienced it in real life, think about the feeling that comes over you when you see one person sacrifice for another. I firmly believe that this feeling tells us that, deep down, we are created to put people first. I believe this principle is so at our core that we can't help but admire it and praise it when we see it lived out.

Maybe Zig Ziglar put it best when he said this about the *People First* mind-set: "You can have everything in life you want if you will just help other people get what they want." Intrigued? Then follow the example of people who have a high Grit Factor and make *People First* a core principle of your life, your business, and your relationships. If you do, sure enough, over time, you'll be shocked by the dramatic impact this *People First* principle has on growing not only your finances, but your marriage, your friendships, and every other aspect of your life.

Leadership Is Earned

Through the years I've seen over and over again that as a result of putting people first, we earn the right to lead.

And John Maxwell has said, "Leadership is influence—nothing more, nothing less." The twenty-first-century leadership master has spoken! Leadership is influence, period. So when we talk about influence, we're talking about leadership. And vice versa. I've never met a super achiever who said in public or in private, "I did it all by myself!" Instead, it's always the opposite. "I had a great team behind me," they'll say. Just as it takes a village to raise a child, it takes a *team* to win a championship. Similarly, your success will involve other people and all of you going in the same direction. As Henry Ford put it, "If everyone is moving forward together, then success takes care of itself." But for that collaboration to happen, there must be leadership. There must be influence.

Unfortunately, many individuals have no influence. Zero. Leading others is as impossible for them as herding cats because they aren't leading their own lives well! They can't seem to get themselves—much less anyone else—moving in the right direction. All the time I see good-hearted and well-intentioned individuals start a small business or begin a sales career. They quickly get frustrated when no one is buying what they're selling, and they look for someone or something to blame. "The product labeling isn't good enough," they'll say. Or "The website is too slow!" Those aren't the real issues, but the truth is not what most of these people want to hear.

Meanwhile, someone selling the same product or managing the same kind of business is welcoming customers and clients like crazy! People are coming to her. She's like a magnet, drawing customers to her business with invisible ease! These men and women are your super achievers, and they instinctively understand gaining influence takes time. And doing this requires what I call the 4-Stage Process.

The 4-Stage Process

Although super achievers do much naturally and intuitively, they as well as not-yet-super achievers can benefit from this process for creating influence:

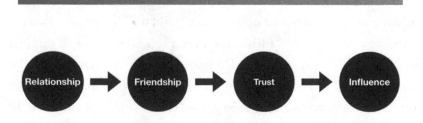

Stage 1: Relationship. So, you meet someone and say hi. You see him occasionally. You know his name; he might know yours. You smile; he smiles. You comment about the weather. It's a friendly enough exchange, but it's completely superficial. You and most of your social media "friends" are at this stage.

Stage 2: Friendship. You've invested time in this person. You've done some things together. You share values and beliefs. This stage is best defined by Shakespeare: "A friend is one that knows you as you are, understands where you have been, accepts what you have become, and still, gently allows you to grow." I can't imagine anyone coming up with a better definition!

Stage 3: Trust. I believe trust is the result of a person's consistency and integrity, meaning all your parts are consistent with the whole. You are who you say you are. You're authentic. You aren't boring; you're steady. You're not unpredictable; you're reliable. You've been tested over time, and you've come through consistently. "It takes twenty years to build a reputation and five minutes to ruin it," billionaire philanthropist Warren Buffett said, talking about trust and consistency. It takes time to build trust, but beware! This stage is fragile! Trust can be so easily broken! Just one inconsistency—one lie, one half-truth, one letdown— and your relationship could be sent back to Stage 1!

Stage 4: Influence. Leaders are made, not born. When people grant you the right to be a leader in their life, they are giving you a gift. When individuals choose me as their leader and allow me to influence them, they're honoring me with their trust. Now, many people hear *leadership* and immediately think of a position or a job title. That would be leadership by position; I'm talking about leadership by permission. The first kind of leadership is given to someone; the other is granted by the followers. Real influence occurs when those being led allow the leader to lead them. When your relationship reaches Stage 3, the other person grants permission for you to lead them, to influence them. But this can only happen after you've done the Stage 3 task of securing trust.

The 4-Stage Process: An Example

Let's go back now to that new entrepreneur who wasn't making any sales. Did the 4-Stage Process help you clearly see the problem? That person was trying to jump from Stage 1 to Stage 4, to go from a purely superficial acquaintance/relationship connection (Stage 1) all the way to the trust necessary to influencing people (Stage 4). Remember, *people don't care how much you know... until they know how much you care.*

On an even more basic level, every relationship falls into one of two categories: relational or transactional. If it's relational, then you're somewhere in the 4-Stage Process, moving closer to trust and influence. If it's transactional, you're not in the process at all! You're sidelined, self-injured by the mind-set *What can this person do for me?* You're not putting people first; you're putting you first! There is no relationship. It's just you, and other people are your vending machines!

So back to the 4-Stage Process. How can you tell what stage your relationship is in? Well, there is a very simple test to find out. Simply send a text message and you'll know immediately! Text your "friend" the following: *Hey, let's get together.* Then wait for the reply. No reply or *Sure, but what about?!...* Not good. You're still in Stage 1. However, if the reply is *Absolutely! When and where?!...* Bingo! You're at Stage 3, maybe even Stage 4!

Leadership or Management?

All super achievers are leaders—and effective leaders tend to be super achievers. Actually, effective leaders *must* be super achievers in order to get everyone moving in the same direction toward a common goal. Yet individuals with a high Grit Factor are always leading with their actions and, therefore, often leading without knowing it. Their ability to influence comes from who they are and what they have done. These people are doers, and their actions, over time, give their words value. People will not only listen but also trust what they say!

Now, as I close this chapter, let me offer a special warning about what I call "positional control." This kind of leadership is assigned: someone gets a title like Manager, Supervisor, Vice President, or Galactic Starship Commander. Merely having a title, though, doesn't make you a leader. A title also doesn't mean that you have influence. Remember, *leadership is gift given by the follower.*

So, beware of getting a title and only some positional control! I've never heard anyone say they want to be managed. Therefore don't sit back in your swivel chair and expect others to act when you're not out front leading the charge! People don't do what you say; they do what you do. Your team will follow the example that you set with your behavior. Will you be a leader—out in front, taking action, growing your organization? Or will you be the uninspiring manager?

Let me tell you, managers are a dime a dozen. To be a leader, to be a person of influence, takes *grit*—and that's a currency hard to come by. But if you'll follow the 4-Stage Process, soon enough you'll be like that magnetic salesperson! Customers and clients will be flocking to your door, calling you on your phone, asking to buy! Because they *trust* you.

Action Steps to Increase Your Grit Factor

- Make a list of the people in your group (business, team, family, etc.). Next to each name, write down what that person wants in life. What are their bullseyes? What can you do to help them hit their bullseyes? If you don't know what some of your people want, take time to sit down with each of them to find out exactly what they're looking for and how you can help them achieve it.

- What are some ways you can start putting other people first? Write down as many ideas as you can. Be specific—and choose one to act on today.

- Avoid people who talk only about themselves. Find and associate with winners, with individuals who have a team-first attitude!

- What value are you adding to the lives of people in your sphere of influence? Are you truly being relational, or are you being transactional? Do you look to add value to people, or do you look for what people can do for you?

- Write down a list of people you do life with. Then, next to each name, note which stage—Relationship, Friend, Trust, Influence—you are in with that person.

- Associate with influential people. Reading biographies and autobiographies counts. Watch videos. If at all possible, spend as much time as possible around these people.

- Having spent some time thinking about putting people first, revisit your six bullseyes. Applying your new understanding and self-awareness, update the Downhill Habits. Then add to or fine-tune the Uphill Habits that will replace the Downhill and enable you to be more selfless in all aspects of life.

Chapter 13
PURPOSE

*The two most important days in life are the day you were born and
the day you discover the reason why.*
—Mark Twain

P eriodically I do a Celebrity Guest Q&A for various LoganStout.
com offerings and events. I welcome a variety of people—from
business moguls like Grant Cardone, to best-selling authors,
Hall of Fame athletes, and others—and the Q&As are live, unscripted,
unrehearsed—and definitely worthwhile. Recently I welcomed Jonathan
Scott, a ten-year NFL veteran and college national champion at the
University of Texas. I consider Jonathan much more than a business
partner; he's truly a friend.

Even so, I treated Jonathan the way I treat all my guests. I didn't
give my buddy any kind of heads-up about what to expect. My guests

have no idea what I'm going to ask, so I know their answers will be authentic and real for the viewers. So here is just one question and one answer from that incredible interview with Jonathan Scott:

Me: You played ten years in the NFL, and then you successfully transitioned into a great business career. Many people watching this have either gone through, are going through, or will go through a transitional period of their own—and it's tough. Tell us how you were able to make that transition so smoothly.

Jonathan: First, I have to give credit to my parents who instilled in me humility. They also taught me that there are cycles in life, that everything comes in seasons.

During our football careers, from middle school to high school to college and into the pros, we [athletes] get all this attention. But what happens is, when our career is over, that attention is *gone*! So, most guys go through a mourning process. There comes an inner conflict where you're saying to yourself, *I'm not good anymore. I'm not valuable anymore. I'm not worth anything.* And depression sets in.

But for me, I'd always had in the back of my mind that there was going to be an end to football. My dad had always told me, "Son, when you get older and you have a little money in your pocket, incorporate yourself!" *Incorporating yourself* didn't mean go get a job. To me, it meant finding your purpose. What's my purpose?

So, my making a smooth transition meant me having moments of silence. I'd ask myself, *OK, what's my purpose?* I would sit still, and I'd ask God repeatedly, "Why am I here? What am I here for?"

The answer that I got was *I am here to empower people.* Empower people. That's my purpose. So I use my platform, my success in football, as a way to empower people.

To sum it all up, when you're going through a transition, find what your purpose is. For me to find my purpose, it took silence along with a conversation with God.

We can all learn from Jonathan!

And, yes, Jonathan does have a high Grit Factor. He is self-motivated—intrinsically motivated—to accomplish and achieve. Jonathan and other high-Grit-Factor individuals don't need a boss looking over their shoulder. Their motivation doesn't come from a feel-good movie, the *Rocky* soundtrack, or the alarm waking them up with "Eye of the Tiger" blaring. They know that kind of motivation doesn't last. Instead, high-Grit-Factor people are self-motivated because they have a strong sense of their purpose in life. They have a reason *why* they do what they do—and their *why* is big!

If you recall the discussion back in Chapter 9: your passions are what you absolutely *love* doing more than anything. Your talents are what you are *really* good at. And…:

The following truths will help you find your purpose and ultimately fulfill as much of your potential as possible:

1. You can be, do, and have more.
2. Pursuing your purpose will 100 percent require making sacrifices.

3. The sacrifice *is* worth it
4. The people you allow in your life will make or break you. They either keep you stuck or help you grow.
5. Reaching your potential is a process. It will take time, and it requires a plan.
6. Success rarely, if ever, happens without perseverance. Stick with your goal of fulfilling your potential!

It's All About the Why

When mentoring people who are venturing out into something new—be it entrepreneurship, solopreneurship, a new marriage, or anything else—I immediately ask questions to discover their *why*. What's their purpose? Why are they doing what they're doing? I also tell them up front about the challenges that lie ahead in their new endeavor. And I'm very honest with them: "Look, obstacles will come, and if your why isn't bigger than your obstacles, you'll quit!" It's my job as their leader, coach, and mentor to know their purpose and prepare them for what lies ahead. So, when those obstacles do come up—and they always do—I'm able if necessary to quickly remind them of their *why*. Never forget why you started in the first place.

In addition, I recommend to the people I mentor that they be able to communicate their *why* to others. As Simon Sinek asserted in his book *Start with Why*, "People don't buy *what* you do; they buy *why* you do it!" Who cares what you're selling? People want to know why you're selling it. What's the purpose behind your actions? What is my new client or my new teammate's *why*? I find out. And can my client and teammate communicate their *why* to others? That's just as important.

And consider this. In 1978, a Harvard professor of psychology named Ellen Langer published her research about the power of the word *because*.

Langer had people request to break in on a line of people waiting to use a busy copy machine on a college campus. (This is before personal printers, when lines were long for using the copy machine.) The researchers had the people use three differently scripted requests to break in line:

"Excuse me, I have five pages. May I use the Xerox machine?"

"Excuse me, I have five pages. May I use the Xerox machine *because* I have to make copies?"

"Excuse me, I have five pages. May I use the Xerox machine *because* I'm in a rush?"

So, did the wording affect whether people let them break in line? Here are the crazy results!

60% compliance

93% compliance!!!

94% compliance!!!

Clearly there is a dramatic difference in the result when we use the powerful word *because*!

Based on this example, more recent books on the subject of purpose, and my own experience, I can tell you with certainty: *why* you do something matters more than *what* you do. The real power of the word *because* is that it introduces the *why.* People are typically more interested in the *why* than the *what*!

Knowing Your *Why*

People may be interested in your *why*, but your *why* is an absolute lifeline for you. Knowing why you're doing something will enable you to persevere through the challenges and stay at it for the long haul. You have to be clear on your *why.* You must know your purpose.

Recently, a single mother approached me at one of my Leadership Summits. "Logan, I've lost my purpose," she said. "My two daughters have both graduated and left the house. I feel I've lost my purpose of being the mother they once needed."

With a smile, I responded, "You haven't lost your purpose. You've just confused your identity."

I have only one critical guideline for you: your purpose must be bigger than you. Your *why* must reach far beyond just yourself. In fact, you may more easily define your *why* if you ask, *Who?* Ask yourself, *Who is counting on me?* Ask yourself: *Who will benefit from me achieving my goal?* Or even: *How can I help millions of people?* Questions like these help you think beyond yourself. Your answers will broaden your *why* and strengthen your purpose. We'll talk about legacy later, but ask yourself: *What do I want my legacy to be? Will my kids' kids' kids know my name? What will they think of me?*

Will you be that person who changed the course of life for your family forever?

Fueling Your Resolve

Finally, whatever your purpose is, I encourage you to set up your environment to remind you of your *why*. Posting your bullseyes where you can see them every day is a start. Be sure to have other positive visuals throughout your day that remind you why you are doing all you do. For example, I put a picture of my twin boys on my cellphone because Miles and Cooper are a huge part of my *why*. You can do the same. You can put your vision board where you can see it several times a day, or maybe photos of the people counting on you will remind and encourage you. And you always rely on your bathroom mirror.

These environmental cues are crucial to you living out your purpose. Why do I believe that? Because in the fog of war, we can easily forget why we're fighting. By making these reminders part of your environment, your *why* remains bigger and greater than any obstacle you encounter. Your *why* fuels your resolve to do whatever it takes to pursue your purpose no matter how bad things get. A small *why* may mean a very small probability of success just as a huge *why* could lead to a huge success!

Action Steps to Increase Your Grit Factor:

- Take quiet time to be alone. Ask yourself: *What is my purpose? What is the reason I'm here?*
- List those individuals who are counting on you. What impact will your success have on their lives? If you don't succeed, what will happen to them?
- Put up reminders of your *why*. On your desk, on your phone, on the fridge, in the car, in the bathroom—have reminders of your *why* everywhere.
- Think about which of the 5 Stages—Stage 1: Honeymoon, Stage 2: Adversity, Stage 3: Progress, Stage 4: Management Mode, Stage 5: Success—you are in with your various roles, jobs, relationships, etc. Remember *why* you started each in the first place and determine what you need to do to get to Stage 5 in all of them!
- Having spent some time thinking about your purpose in life, revisit your six bullseyes. Applying your new understanding and self-awareness, update the Downhill Habits. Then add to or fine-tune the Uphill Habits that will replace the Downhill and enable you to work more toward your purpose in all aspects of life.

Chapter 14

INTEGRITY

Power is actualized when word and deed have not parted company.
—Hannah Arendt

I f you owned a business—or maybe you already do—and were looking
to hire an individual or bring on a new teammate, what would you
look for in that person? What qualities would you want him or her to
have? A good attitude, possibly? A strong work ethic? Charisma? When
asked the same question by a Nebraska business magazine, the very
successful Warren Buffett said this:

> You're looking for three things, generally, in a person:
> intelligence, energy, and integrity. But if they don't have the last
> one, don't even bother with the first two.

Wow. So no matter how smart the applicants are and no matter how much energy they have, if they lack *integrity*, Warren doesn't want 'em.

So what is this all-important component, *integrity*? This is how Webster's defines it:

> *Integrity*: the quality or state of being complete or undivided; completeness

I'd like to make it simple: You have integrity when what you *do* and what you *say* are what you *believe*! *Integrity* means that your words and your actions are *aligned* with your beliefs.

So what are your beliefs? With what truths and values do you want to align your words and actions? These beliefs, truths, and values that you hold are quite relevant to determining and then to hitting your bullseyes in all six aspects of life. Simply put, integrity is necessary to staying on course with your goals. If you live without integrity, the world will beat you down, and you'll easily start chasing what it values, money, fame, recognition, and more.

Remember NFL star Jonathan Scott from the previous chapter? In a quiet conversation with God, he found his purpose: he realized that he was on this planet to empower people. Jonathan is a man of integrity: his work, his words, and his actions are completely aligned with that purpose. This alignment—this consistency—show his integrity.

With integrity, you—like Jonathan—will stay true to *who* you are and *whose* you are!

Integrity Tested

Adding an important point about integrity, Oprah Winfrey said, "Real integrity is doing the right thing knowing that nobody is going to know if you did it or not." I absolutely agree. It's imperative to live in alignment even if *no one* is watching. In fact, it's integrity *only* if your work, words, and actions are aligned with your values and beliefs even when no one is watching.

Sadly, we've all seen people who act and speak one way in front of certain people but act and speak completely different in another setting and—the conclusion is easily drawn—when no one is watching. These people lack integrity: their words, actions, values, and beliefs are obviously not in alignment. And you've probably heard individuals talk a big game, but then saw that their actions didn't back up their words. Again, these out-of-alignment individuals lack integrity.

Such inconsistency between conduct and conversation creates a constant internal conflict that these people may not even be aware of. Whether or not these individuals are aware, the existence of this conflict between words and actions is guaranteed to prevent them from being their best and, ultimately, will lower their Grit Factor considerably. Furthermore, without integrity, people lose the drive to finish what they start, and they certainly won't do things with excellence. Rather, they simply go through the motions.

One way of going through the motions at work is doing a job simply for the money. These workers don't necessarily believe in what they are providing, selling, or promoting. I get it. I've been there! And if you're there now, don't stay there! Do life with integrity, and life will be better.

And I say that life will be better because integrity brings wholeness and inner peace. Integrity doesn't make us perfect, but it can purify our intentions and motives. Doing life with integrity—the assignment is simple to understand, but it's not always easy to live out.

If what you do and what you say don't align with what you actually believe, know you do have the power to change that.

Action Steps to Increase Your Grit Factor

- Ask yourself—and/or God and/or a spouse or trusted friend— "Are my words and my actions in alignment with my beliefs?" If not, why do you think that's the case—and what will you do to become a person of greater integrity?

- What actions could you start doing that would be in alignment with your beliefs? Write those down. Consider why you haven't done these things before so you can avoid those pitfalls as you build your integrity.

- Having spent some time thinking about integrity, revisit your six bullseyes. Applying your new understanding and self-awareness, update the Downhill Habits. Then add to or fine-tune the Uphill Habits that will replace the Downhill and enable you to live with integrity in every aspect of your life.

Chapter 15

RELENTLESSNESS

Opportunity is missed by most people because it is dressed in overalls and looks like work.

—Thomas Edison

"Achieving my dreams was easier than I ever imagined," said no one ever! Remember, the pursuit is going to be hard, and you will get knocked down. That's why individuals who achieve success—those who have a high Grit Factor—show themselves to be absolutely relentless.

Boxer Mike Tyson, who's certainly had his ups and downs, said, "Everyone has a plan until they get punched in the face." Trust me, as soon as you venture out to start climbing Success Mountain, punches will come from all directions—from family, "friends," relatives, coworkers. The prisoners don't want to see another prisoner escape! Like crabs in a bucket, they'll do all they can to pull you down and try to stop you.

How will you respond to the punches? You've been warned that they're coming. You understand that you'll need to be *relentless* to push on!

Fall Down? Get Up!

Before I go further, I want to clear up a big misconception: I believe most people—usually those on the sidelines of life, who aren't taking any action whatsoever—look at those who have reached the peak of Success Mountain and assume every day is a good day for those individuals. In addition, those successful individuals are seen as lucky, possibly superhuman, or somehow above the day-to-day struggles of life. It appears that everything they touch turns to gold as they keep crushing their goals. Let me assure you, however, that every human being has tough days. After all, we're human!

Every single person on the planet and throughout history has tough days, and every single person gets knocked down by life. And reaching the top of Success Mountain doesn't mean those people didn't have down days, and it doesn't mean they'll never again have down days. Scaling that mountain means these folks *don't stay down for long.* They are relentless! When they get knocked down, it's just a matter of time before they get back up even more fired up than when they started. They use all the reasons why their venture won't work to fuel their determination, not kill them. They exemplify what Winston Churchill said: "Success consists of going from failure to failure without loss of enthusiasm."

Seasons of life can indeed feel like movement from failure to failure, but do you realize it only takes *one* big win for you to be a success? And at that moment of achievement, no one cares about your losses and setbacks, however many they may be. For instance, everyone recognizes the numerous baseball world championships I've had in my career—and they seem to have forgotten all the losses I endured as I forged a winning program!

And sports are full of examples of losses being forgotten. No one cares that Babe Ruth set the all-time record for the most strikeouts. He's Babe Ruth, the Great Bambino, the Sultan of Swat! And apparently he didn't care about all those strikeouts either. These are the Babe's own words: "Every strike brings me closer to my next home run!" Clearly, the mind-set of a relentless winner! Basketball player extraordinaire Michael Jordan, same thing:

> I've missed more than 9000 shots in my career. I've lost almost 300 games. [And] 26 times, I've been trusted to take the game-winning shot and missed. I've failed over and over and over again in my life. And that is why I succeed.
> Relentlessness.

From Setback to Comeback

In the past few decades, perhaps one of the greatest stories of being relentless is the story of Sylvester Stallone. He went through a lot of adversity to achieve his goal of being a Hollywood actor.

Just after he was born, he suffered from a paralyzed bottom jaw, and as a result he slurred his words. When Stallone started auditioning, Hollywood agents would literally laugh at how he spoke. He was rejected more than a thousand times! But, he later said, "I take rejection as someone blowing a bugle in my ear to wake me up and get going, rather than retreat." So he kept going, but the struggles continued. At one point, he was even homeless, and he lived in a bus terminal for three weeks. Then he hit his lowest point: he had to *sell* his only friend—his dog—to a stranger at a liquor store because he couldn't afford to feed his loyal companion. He cried hard that day as he walked away from his beloved dog.

But we all know the happy ending to Sylvester Stallone's story. Yes, life hit him in the face more than a thousand times, but he kept getting back up. Maybe that's why the role of Rocky fit him so well. The gritty fighter who refused to stay down was Stallone's story on camera! And since the first *Rocky* movie, no one has cared about all the times he got rejected. He's Sylvester Stallone! He's *Rocky*!

When individuals like Sylvester Stallone—individuals who have a high Grit Factor—experience a setback, they take a step back, and they're ready for their comeback!

Guaranteed!

As a leader, it's my responsibility to prepare you for what's ahead. I guarantee that you *will* get knocked down. The journey *will* be hard. But hear me on this: Not only should you expect the challenges, but I guarantee that persevering will be absolutely worth it in the end. Everything in life that is truly worthwhile takes longer, costs more, and is a lot harder than you ever imagined—and that's how you know you're on the right track!

In *A League of Their Own,* the coach—played by Tom Hanks—says to the player who wants to quit, "It's supposed to be hard. If it weren't hard, everyone would do it. The hard is what makes it great."

Every single baseball season I've coached has had its tough patches. My job as the leader was not only to create relentless players, but to be a relentless coach. Being that kind of coach wasn't always easy. You know, I don't recall a season in my career when I didn't give the *We didn't come this far to not win the World Series* speech. And the same holds true in business. In every single company I've either invested in or started, we reached a moment when we could either close the doors or put our heads down and work harder than ever before. And the *hard* is what makes the victory, the success, the goal achieved *great.*

All In!

And because the pursuit of a win or a goal is hard, you must be relentless. *Relentless* implies never quitting. In fact, quitting isn't even on the radar! *Relentless* implies having no other choice but to succeed.

I'll win, or I'll die trying becomes your level of commitment. *Relentless* means, as Jim Rohn put it, "I will climb this mountain. They told me it is too high, too far, too steep, too rocky, and too difficult. But it's my mountain. I will climb it! Soon, you will see me waving from the top or dead on the side! 'Cause I ain't coming back!"

The reality is, most people are *not* relentless. Instead of pushing ahead, they give themselves a way out of a situation. Truly successful people—the truly relentless people—burn the boats. They never consider quitting or turning back. They keep their eyes forward, locked on their bullseyes! Truly successful people understand that they are all in or all out! There's no such thing as a toe in the water. Relentless people don't say, "Let's try and see how it goes." Heck no! They dive in! In fact, they don't wait for their ship to come in. They swim out to it!

Listen: You are put on this earth to do great things. To win. To dominate. So be bold. Be brave. Be relentless... and *win*!

Action Steps to Increase Your Grit Factor

- Experience isn't the great teacher. *Evaluated* experience is the great teacher. Don't live in the past but learn from it. What would your life look like if you had been more relentless? Where could you have pushed further, harder, stronger, and then probably hit the mark?
- Now consider what you have in front of you. What lesson(s) from your evaluated experience will you apply to a given situation or, perhaps, to your life in general?
- What are three ways you can be more relentless in pursuit of one of your goals? Be specific—and then get started on one.
- Having spent some time thinking about relentlessness, revisit your six bullseyes. Applying your new understanding and self-awareness, update the Downhill Habits. Then add to or

fine-tune the Uphill Habits that will replace the Downhill and enable you to be focused and relentless in every aspect of your life.

Chapter 16
ATTITUDE

A positive attitude starts a chain reaction of positive thoughts, events, and outcomes. It is a catalyst, and it sparks extraordinary results.

—Wade Boggs

E arlier in the book I touched on the importance of having a positive attitude and surrounding yourself with positive people. I want to revisit this topic and give it the attention it deserves. And attitude is definitely worthy of attention. Did you know that most people lose their jobs, their influence, and even some life-changing opportunities due to a lack of positive attitude? Very few people are fired due to a lack of ability. The more frequent reason for firing someone is that person's negative outlook and attitude.

My Law of Attraction

When we're talking about attitude, here's the bottom line: We attract who we are. More to the point, *you* attract who *you* are. It's not that we attract *who* we want. Nor do we attract *what* we want. Rather, we attract *who* we *are*. We attract *what* we *are*. To be specific, positive attracts positive. Negative attracts negative. Like attracts like. This is my Law of Attraction.

Let me tell you a quick true story of a young man whose grandmother was concerned because he hadn't yet settled down with a serious girlfriend or a wife. Sitting him down, Grandma said, "I'm worried about you. Why don't you have a girlfriend or even a wife at this point? After all, it's lonely to be alone."

He responded thoughtfully, "Grandma, on a scale of one to ten—with ten being the best—I'd rank myself as a six. I know the life principle that I attract who I *am*, not who I *want*. So if I want a woman who is a nine or even a ten, I must first improve myself so that I'm a nine or a ten."

The grandmother smiled at her grandson's wisdom. She agreed.

First Things First

I also agree with that young man, and I call the conclusion he arrived at *alignment before assignment*. I believe you must first be aligned within yourself. You must get *you* right first. But most people have it backward. They wake up and walk out the door every morning looking to work on others and to somehow better the world by doing so. They fail to first work on and better themselves.

Similarly, entrepreneurs, sellers, bankers, agents—they're all looking for people to join their business or buy their product. They want enthusiastic buyers. They want high-class clients. They want business-minded associates. But have they looked in the mirror and asked themselves: *Am I the type of person who would attract a buyer/client/*

associate like that? To quote Madonna, "If you want to change the world, first change yourself."

If you want to attract positive people into your business, be positive! You want to attract passionate and excited customers? OK, be passionate and excited! You want a friend? First be a friend! It's that simple. You attract who you *are*.

World-class achievers not only know this, but they embrace it and they live it. Before they can have around them the people they want, they know they must first *become*.

The Most Contagious Force in the World

My wife and I were elated when Miles and Cooper were born. During the first several months of their lives, we were extremely careful about keeping them healthy. No one who was sick got near our boys, and anyone who held our boys had just washed their hands. We did our best to protect them from the contagious germs others might carry.

Most people take similar measures to protect their own body from illness and disease, but very few pay much attention to protecting their *mind*. That concerns me because I believe the most contagious force in the world is *not* a germ or a disease. I believe the most contagious force in the world is a negative attitude. Nothing spreads as fast as negativity!

I've experienced this—and maybe you have—on conference calls and in business meetings countless times. Leaders come together to share good ideas. But then, out of the blue, one person shares something negative, and suddenly the agenda is out the window, the meeting is now a gripe fest, and the mood of the whole group has gone *sour* fast!

I believe the reason for this is, it's much easier to be negative than positive. The musician Chuck D said this:

Being positive is like going up a mountain. Being negative is like sliding down a hill. A lot of times, people want to take the easy way out, because it's basically what they've understood throughout their lives.

So true. Negativity is definitely a slippery slope. The smallest little bit can instantly send you sliding down Success Mountain!

Knowing this, I will run—literally run—from negative people! You know the types. Gossipers. Whiners. Complainers. I can't get away fast enough! Engaging with them is like Brer Rabbit touching the Tar Baby! Run! Get away!

Most people, however, sit, smile, and listen. They tacitly approve the negativity by not saying anything in response. They simply sit and allow the negativity to seep into their minds, not realizing the effect the negativity is having on their character and their potential success. Negativity erodes a person's Grit Factor. And negativity is clear, indisputable evidence that we live in a fallen world. Negativity comes from all directions—friends, family, the environment, TV, other media. The list goes on. Yet the successful person—that individual with a high Grit Factor—stays positive. How can we stay positive in a negative world?

Darren Hardy, best-selling author, former editor of *Success Magazine,* and a good friend, answers this question with a powerful analogy in his book *The Compound Effect.* Darren says—and I'm paraphrasing—that your mind is like a glass of crystal-clear water. The negative world is nasty black sludge that drips constantly into your clear water. Drip… drip… drip… The negativity constantly drips into your mind. Darren says that the secret to keeping the water clear—to keeping your mind clear—is to flush your glass daily with *clean* water. You flush your mind through such personal development activities as reading and praying. You must intentionally and daily flush your mind and fill it with good. We're back to the importance of you developing you!

Like Attracts Like

Just as negative thoughts attract more negative thoughts, positive thoughts attract more positive thoughts. And people can have the same effect as thoughts do: positive people attract positive people. So think about the people in your life today. Are they negative? Or are they positive? What you notice could be a good indication of who *you* are as a person.

I'll never forget the time I had just finished speaking at a conference, and during the meet-and-greet session afterwards (which I genuinely love), a woman about fifty years old handed me a copy of my book *Stout Advice* to sign and began explaining why she hasn't ever been successful.

"Mr. Stout, I truly want to be successful. I've read your book twice, I attend every event of yours that I can, but I simply can't avoid negative people. They seem to flock to me!"

She continued for two minutes before my staff kindly reminded her that hundreds of people were patiently waiting, and that she needed to wrap up. I felt bad for her, but as I was listening, it became 100 percent clear that... *she was the problem*. Negativity oozed out of her, so she was attracting negative people. That poor woman set me up for a huge revelation: *Negative people will never be successful no matter how hard they work*. They may win for a short time, but they'll lose in the long run.

Anyway, that woman is the reason for this chapter. After meeting her, I started studying the attribute of positivity and found that even the least productive people who have a positive attitude last longer at a job than the most productive people who have a bad attitude. Let that sink in! And a productive person who has a positive attitude can lift up and encourage an entire group, team, organization, and company.

And individuals with a high Grit Factor have a positive attitude. They still have to deal with negative forces, real challenges, and life's tragedies and loss, but as I've said, what happens to us is not as significant as how we respond. A positive attitude doesn't mean you're living in a happy fantasy bubble. Having a positive attitude means that you—as Michael Jordan put it—"Always turn a negative situation into a positive situation."

The Choice Is Yours

As I wrap up here, consider this short rhyme:

Two men look out from the same bars.
One sees the mud, the other sees the stars.

Being positive is a choice. It's a daily choice. It's a moment-by-moment choice you make every waking moment of your life. Whatever the mud in your life, the glass can be half full because you choose it to be.

In every situation, will you look at the bad—or will you find the good? In every quiet moment, will you think about the bad—or will you think about the good? A positive attitude is a perpetual choice that each of us can make.

Know that I'm positive you can be and will be… positive!

Action Steps to Increase Your Grit Factor:

- Who are the negative people in your life? What can you do to *limit* or perhaps even *end* your associations with these negative people?
- Who are the positive people in your life? What steps will you take to *increase* the time you spend with these positive people?
- What negative environments (locations, events, etc.) should you avoid in order to avoid negative people?
- What positive environments (church, leadership events, etc.) will you visit more consistently?

- What groups (networking groups, social groups, etc.) could you join that would place you around positive people?
- What Uphill Habits could you adopt that would fill your mind with positivity?
- Having spent some time thinking about your attitude, revisit your six bullseyes. Applying your new understanding and self-awareness, update the Downhill Habits. Then add to or fine-tune the Uphill Habits that will replace the Downhill and enable you to be more positive in every aspect of your life.

Chapter 17

FINANCIAL MOTIVATION

Money is a terrible master, but an excellent servant.
—**P. T. Barnum**

To be honest, I hesitated putting this chapter in the book. The phrase *financial motivation* seems so worldly and superficial. So why is the chapter here? Because if I were to ask anyone on the planet, "Would you rather get paid ten thousand a year for your job or ten thousand a day for your job?" the answer would overwhelmingly be the latter.

And one reason is that, from the world's perspective, three things are necessary for genuine freedom in life: time, money, and health. Remove any one of those three, and you are *not* free. You can have all kinds of time and good health, but without money you are limited. You can have all the money and time in the world, but without good health you are limited. And you can be healthy and have money, but without time to enjoy it, you are limited. It takes that trifecta to be free.

Zig Ziglar famously said, "Money isn't the most important thing in life, but it's reasonably close to oxygen on the must-have list." Individuals with a high Grit Factor—the super achievers of this world—have a proper understanding of money, and they recognize the direct connection between having money and fulfilling their purpose. As deeply driven to fulfill their purpose as they are, these individuals with a high Grit Factor are nevertheless and absolutely financially motivated. And I don't think that's a bad thing.

The Bible says, "The love of money is the root of all evil" (1 Timothy 6:10). Notice it's the "*love* of money"—not money itself—that's the root of all evil. That's an important distinction. This verse teaches that money should never be the end goal. Instead, money should remain simply a means of achieving that goal.

Value First!

What is money? Have you ever stopped and thought about it? Simply put, money is what we exchange for *value*. In other words, when value is given, money is received. We are paid for bringing value to the marketplace. If we bring a lot of value, then we rightfully receive a lot of money. If we bring little value, then we rightfully receive little money. It's that simple, but of course there are exceptions.

I, for instance, have a background in ministry as well as coaching. I assure you I was *extremely* underpaid as a minister and as a college baseball coach. My mother-in-law was a teacher, and teachers are severely underpaid despite their key role in shaping the next generation and our society. I have friends who serve and protect us as law enforcement, firefighters, and paramedics. These individuals provide life-changing and sometimes lifesaving value, yet—relatively speaking—get paid very little in return. Then again, we signed up for that calling; we knew what we were getting into. So back to the point.

Consider a doctor who can operate on the rarest of brain diseases. He or she will receive a lot of money in exchange for the value they bring to the operating room. Furthermore, this value they offer took years, often decades, to develop. Over time and with ongoing education, hands-on training, multiple degrees, countless books, and perhaps his own research, this doctor is definitely high value in the marketplace.

Sadly, most but not all people who have little or no money have brought little or no value to the marketplace. Frankly, these individuals offer little that the marketplace would consider valuable. Now, could they still be a valuable parent? Yes! And are they still valuable in the sight of God? Absolutely! But in the marketplace, they offer little skill, talent, knowledge, or experience to exchange for the money they want. Not understanding this, most people resort to asking, "How can I get more money?" But what they should be asking is "How can I give more value?" Value must be given first! Then money will come.

Potential and Expansion

Motivational speaker Jim Rohn often said to his audiences, "How tall does a tree grow?" Later in his talk he'd answer his question: "A tree will always grow... as tall as it can!" Then he challenged his audience to be *all they can be*. That's also a U.S. Army advertising slogan: *Be All You Can Be!* I absolutely agree with that call to action.

That said, I believe what weighs most on people as they enter their retirement years is... unfulfilled potential. The pain of sacrifice is far easier to endure than the pain of regret. My purpose in life is to help others reach their God-given potential in all six areas of life—mental, physical, spiritual, financial, emotional, and relational—and these six are all connected. Weakness in one area brings down the other five. So you absolutely must, for instance, have your finances in order if you expect to fulfill your mental, physical, spiritual, emotional, and relational potential.

By this point, I hope you're saying to yourself, *I get it, Logan. So what must I do to have more money?* I have three suggestions and a bonus tip:

1. **Decide that money is important** to fulfilling your purpose. Be sure you can answer these questions: *What is my purpose? How much money do I need to fulfill my purpose?* and *Who is counting on me to do exactly that?* I'm sure your answers will put the fire in your belly to earn more money, yet money will be kept in its proper place: it's a means, not an end.

2. **Make yourself more valuable**. We find ourselves back to a core idea in this book: personal development. *You* must develop *you*. What skill can you do better than most? What steps could you take to improve that skill? your communication skills? your time management skills? What problems that people have can you provide a solution for? What might you do to serve other people?

3. **Have multiple streams of income** if you, for instance, want to overcome multiple streams of debt. What additional part-time job could you do? Even better what home-based business you can get involved in? Increase the number of your income sources—and researching options is a more effective use of your time than cutting coupons. Also, I'm a *huge* believer in establishing residual income, also referred to as passive income. Be creative as you explore possible sources.

And now the promised bonus.

Due Diligence

If you want to get a raise at work, I'm going to give you the absolute best way to get one. Let's say your salary is $40,000 and you'd like it to be $45,000. Let's also say your job title is assistant, and you want to become a director in the company. Here's my advice: *Work for the role you want and not for the role you currently have.*

In other words, do your job in such a way that gains everyone's respect. If, for example, you want to be a member of the executive team one day, then think, act, and perform like an executive now. Avoid that "just enough" disease; instead embody the "whatever it takes" attitude in your current role. The person responsible for promoting you is guaranteed to eventually see the value you are adding to the organization.

Most people don't try this approach. They do nothing more than complain that they haven't been promoted. They have a victim mind-set and feel they aren't appreciated and recognized enough. They do nothing to add value to the organization, and the person responsible for promoting will notice that as well.

I once owned an investment company that gave entrepreneurs opportunities to pitch their business. If I liked the particular business, we would come to terms and then go to due diligence, the process where most potential investments die. My attorneys would vet everything, and more often than not, what I had been pitched proved not exactly accurate, and I'd have to walk away from the deal.

But in 2014 I was pitched a deal that came very close to passing due diligence. When this happens, I actually tour the existing company's facilities for one last round of due diligence. I want to see everything myself, identify any points of concern, and look at the business from a personnel standpoint. I'll never forget this particular acquisition because that day I met one of the greatest teammates I've ever had.

Finding Laura

In this particular acquisition, I actually bought a customized vitamin technology, not an actual company. I would be the one to form a brand-new company. So as I was touring the facility, I was looking to see if there was anything else we needed to complete the acquisition.

After meeting all the staff, I walked out of the building, looked at my legal team, and said, "If I can only have one thing from that office, I have to bring Laura with me!"

Laura did in fact come onboard as a project manager. Her can-do attitude and effort were exactly right for our newly formed company. (Actually, those qualities make an employee right for any position!) No matter what we asked of Laura, she found a way to get the job done—and done with excellence. And in the rare moments when we couldn't hit a deadline, she was honest about it. She told me why a project would be behind and the date it would be delivered. No drama. No surprises. She was consistent day in and day out. She delivered! I could always count on her.

And, although she had never before held an executive-level title in her career, she is—as I write this book—the president of one of the fastest-growing companies on the globe, valued at well over $100 million.

Work for the role you want, and one day you will have the role you deserve.

Stay Focused on the Eternal

It's perfectly normal to be financially motivated to succeed. Just make sure you don't lose sight of your purpose. Keep thinking of money as the means to an end, the end being your fulfillment of your purpose.

It's way too easy to do, but don't get caught up in the flash and dash of money. Most people buy stuff they can't afford… to impress people they don't even know. Don't be that person! Money has a place for sure but keep it in perspective. Dabble in the temporal but stay focused on the eternal.

Now I say this as someone who grew up in a small apartment with my mom and my brother. As a kid, I used to collect cans and bottle caps so I could have a few extra bucks. All that to say, I've been poor—but I've been rich too. And I can say without hesitation that rich is better. Money gives you options. Money can go places and reach people and touch lives. Money builds churches and feeds the homeless. The super-successful know this, and I personally have had some amazing experiences seeing the good that money can do in this world.

I've been honored to receive a lot of awards in my career, but first on my list of proudest moments are the accolades from philanthropies. I'll never forget the first time I was called a "philanthropist." I had been named chair of the American Heart Association Heart Ball as well as, for the second time, honorary chair for the Boys and Girls Club of Collin County—two great nonprofits doing great things. Another highlight of my life was standing on stage with John Maxwell and handing him a check for $200,000 for his nonprofit EQUIP, an organization dedicated to developing Christian leaders. We can't give what we don't have!

Finally, one of the greatest advantages of having money is peace of mind. In my experience, I thought *most* about money at those times when I had *no* money. *How can I pay the rent? How much is this going to cost?* I'd worry. Money consumed my thinking back when I had *none*. Now I do have money, so now I'm more focused on fulfilling my purpose. Money is simply a means to fulfilling that purpose.

And that's the perspective that super achievers have. They are driven by their purpose and being financially motivated helps them be able to fulfill that purpose.

Action Steps to Increase Your Grit Factor

- Describe the connection between income and fulfilling your purpose. Also determine how much money you need to fulfill your purpose.
- Find more sources of income. What job could you do in the hours that seem to slip through your fingers? What small business could you start? What home-based direct-sales company can you join? Explore and then expand!
- Make yourself more valuable to the organization. Every day do one thing (read a book, practice a skill, improve your ability to communicate, etc.) that increases your value in your current job and/or in the general marketplace.
- Having spent some time thinking about the degree to which you are motivated by finances, revisit your six bullseyes. Applying your new understanding and self-awareness, update the Downhill Habits. Then add to or fine-tune the Uphill Habits that will replace the Downhill and enable you to be more financially responsible in every aspect of your life.

Chapter 18
COACHABILITY

Every man I meet is my superior in some way, and in that I learn from him.

—Ralph Waldo Emerson

We all know people who are always "right" even when they're wrong. It's annoying, isn't it? But they *know* they're right. Usually these individuals are the ones always talking, never listening, and invariably ready with a comeback when someone attempts to... uh... coach them. But have you noticed that these folks with lots of words are often broke financially, emotionally, and/or mentally? Broke Uncle Harry has all the answers! It's these people I literally want to grab, shake, and yell, "If you know so much, why are you in your current situation?" These people need a wake-up call!

I think behind all this empty talk, these people—like most people on the planet—quit learning when they stopped going to school. They quit being teachable. They quit being coachable. They put down the books and picked up the TV remote. They got a J.O.B. (stands for "Just Over Broke"), stopped learning, yet now live life claiming to have *all* the answers.

Needless to say this book is for them, but they probably won't read it. Hey, they already have all the answers! This book is, however, for you—a person determined to learn—and I know that about you because you picked up this book and have read this far! As Zig Ziglar said so well, "If you are not willing to learn, no one can help you. If you are determined to learn, no one can stop you!"

And those with a high Grit Factor are absolutely determined to learn.

Willing to Learn and Willing to...

Another word for "determined to learn" is *coachable*. And coachable people have a burning desire to *get better*. They never believe they've arrived. In fact, just the opposite: the more they learn, the more they realize how *little* they actually know—and they want to learn even more. So their learning cycle continues.

Supporting this point is *Inc.* magazine's 2017 survey of the CEOs of its top five hundred companies. *Inc.* discovered that these men and women read four to five books a *month*. Yes, a whopping fifty-two books a year! Now before you say, "Yeah, but I don't have time to read four to five books a week!" Let me stop you. You see, I just don't buy it. The fact is, you're undoubtedly reading that much already anyway—but you're just reading the wrong things.

Another 2017 study, this one done by Telegraph.uk.co, revealed that the average person has five different social media accounts and spends one hour and forty minutes per day on social media! One hour and forty minutes! That is sad! So—as I've said—I do believe in social media, but I believe in *using it* and not getting *used by it*.

But merely reading the books won't do the trick because I believe there are two parts to being coachable:

Reading this book tells me, yes, you're willing to learn! But are you willing to change? Here's where the rubber meets the road.

Many people read books, but only a very small number are willing to make any changes. Very few will actually follow through and work toward their bullseyes. If you're truly willing to change, though, you take action. You read the Action Steps to Increase Your Grit Factor in this book—and you actually do them. Willing to change also means you give up negative friends, shed bad habits, and drop old beliefs. You leave behind your past life, cross the bridge of success, and move toward a completely new life. Your choice to climb Success Mountain means you are willing to change. As Tolstoy said: "Everyone thinks of changing the world, but no one thinks of changing himself."

Again, being coachable means you're willing to change.

A Better Perspective

Motivational speaker Les Brown says, "You can't see the picture when you're in the frame." He's right! Each of us needs someone else to see and then tell us what we're not seeing about ourselves and our life. Simply put, everyone needs a coach. In his book *Aspire*, Kevin Hall talks about how the word *coach* comes from an ancient word for an actual vessel that carried people across water, from *where they were* to *where they wanted to be*. If you wanted to get there, only a coach could take you there.

Knowing that each of us needs a coach raises the questions, "Who should be my coach?" and "How do I find a coach who can take me where I want to go?" Before you race off to hire a business guru or a life coach who has a fancy business card, let me give you a benchmark to help your choice: results. Does this person have sufficient knowledge about the results you're looking for? Has this person ever helped someone achieve the results you're after? Or, ideally, has this person ever been where you want to go?

Quality coaching is key to the success of the Dallas Patriots baseball organization. Every year we hold tryouts, thousands of kids attend, and we end up turning away a lot of good-hearted and talented kids—which is the most emotionally difficult part of the job. And every year I'm absolutely honored by all the parents who have their kids try out with our organization. Many drive more than an hour each way, and some even fly in. The reason they come to us is clear: our coaches who have achieved results. Our coaches are former pro athletes and college stars who have been where in the baseball world these kids want to go. My coaches can take these kids where these kids want to go because these coaches have walked that path.

So when you do choose a coach for your ascent of Success Mountain, do yourself the favor of *not* choosing someone you are comfortable with, someone who lets you stay in your—to be honest—tiny *comfort zone*. You don't want that kind of coach because success requires breaking out of your *comfort zone!* So, find a coach who can prove that he or she has generated the kind of results you're looking for. This person will likely be at least a bit outside your comfort zone—but that's exactly the coach you need.

Let me just say, the difference between a fan and a friend is that a fan tells you what you want to hear while a friend tells you what you need to hear. The right coach will serve as your life friend.

Eat Like a Champ

Here's the real issue: Are you truly willing to be told things you don't want to hear? Are you actually coachable? Most people would rather be showered with praise that can smother them than receive constructive feedback that will save them!

The fact is, people who have found success in every aspect of life were and remain coachable. They realize that no matter how successful they are, they aren't even remotely close to how good they can become. Having the right people in your life will mean getting the right feedback. Honest and therefore often hard-to-hear feedback is the meal of champions, and those with a high Grit Factor eat daily! If you're starving for progress and growth in your life, the people you've surrounded yourself with may be telling you what you *want* to hear rather than what you *need* to hear.

And I know about hearing what I *need* to hear! I started my speaking career in my early twenties. Although I was good, I'm so much better today, but only because I taught my team how to coach me. Initially, every time I finished giving a keynote address or leading a training session, I'd ask my team to give me feedback. At first, they gave the typical responses: *You were great! The crowd really loved it! They will certainly hire you back!* I had to be firm with my team. First I asked them, "How am I supposed to improve with all praise?" Then I said, "I need you to really evaluate my delivery, style, tone, content, and message, and identify specific things I can do better." Let me just say, my team certainly took this to heart! To be honest, at times the feedback hurt a little, but only because it was spot-on.

Choose your feedback team carefully. Members need to have earned the right to give you feedback. They are either where you want to be in an area of life, or they earned your trust because they know and understand you. One very important member of my team is my wife. I'll never forget the time she told me that I sometimes come across as if I'm speaking *at* people rather than *with* people. No one wants to be spoken *at*; we want to be spoken *with*. That perspective can move a speaker from communicating to connecting.

Everyone speaks, some communicate, but the best connect. When that connection is made, the audience laughs, cries, learns, gets motivated, feels inspired, and leaves a better person than they were before they heard you speak. A speaker who connects reaches right into the hearts and minds of every person in the room and transforms lives. That's definitely my goal every time I speak.

When I first started, I was a great communicator, but not the best connector. My growth as a keynote speaker and trainer is the reason I'm asked to speak 365 days a year. And my growth has come because of people who give me regular and honest—sometimes brutally honest— feedback. I'm forever grateful to them! I can't encourage you enough to get a circle of people like that in your life.

Action Steps to Increase Your Grit Factor

- Are you willing to learn? What daily Uphill Habits could you adopt that would accelerate your learning? What Downhill Habits do you need to get rid of?
- Are you willing to change? In what aspects of life are you resisting change? What changes do you know you absolutely need to make? Why aren't you making them?
- Is your environment stimulating your desire to learn and grow? If not, what can you do to improve your environment?

- Which of your associations stimulate your desire to learn and grow? If the list is short or nonexistent, consider options for finding such people and spending time with them.

- Do you have a coach? If so, in what ways has this person helped you achieve your goal(s)? In what ways, if any, has your coach's journey been similar to yours? Why is that helpful—or why could it be helpful? If you don't have a coach, get a coach. For personal coaching inquiries, visit LoganStout.com.

- Having spent some time thinking about how coachable you are, revisit your six bullseyes. Applying your new understanding and self-awareness, update the Downhill Habits. Then add to or fine-tune the Uphill Habits that will replace the Downhill and enable you to be more coachable in every aspect of your life.

Chapter 19

ACTION-ORIENTED

I have been impressed with the urgency of doing. Knowing is not enough; we must apply. Being willing is not enough; we must do.
—Leonardo da Vinci

The world is full of over-hyped underachievers. They attend seminars, leadership events, and motivational summits, but nothing about them, nothing in their lives, seems to change. They've simply added a bunch of great new ideas to their repertoire and maybe some new resolutions like "I will get out of debt!" and "I will change my life!" Their intentions aren't the problem; their failure to act is. Words are good for the moment, but only action is good for the movement! Results don't automatically follow learning. Nothing changes without action.

Perhaps the number one obstacle keeping most people from taking action and reaching their goals is fear, an acronym for False Expectations Appearing Real. The obstacles that stop those people who *do* take action are discouragement and doubt. Fear, discouragement, and doubt keep more people from fulfilling their dreams than just about anything else. These three things will keep you from reaching your potential by paralyzing you. But there is a simple solution to conquering fear, discouragement, and doubt—and that is taking action! In fact, action is such a powerful antidote that the very moment you act, doubts and fears vanish like smoke!

Lesson Learned

I'm a huge believer in entrepreneurship. I also truly believe in the power of direct sales. I own and have owned a wide variety of companies, the majority of which have *not* been direct sales. I want to share a big lesson I've learned.

If you want to get out of debt; work part-time or full-time; create passive income; build a real retirement; work with people you *want* to work with; have fun; and represent something you truly believe in, then you should look no further than direct sales. You can start your own business with practically no initial outlay of cash, and the majority of the systems, groundwork, products, services, and more are already in place. I've invested millions of dollars in various business types in hopes of getting a great return. But with direct sales a person can be profitable the first day and have basically no ongoing costs. I truly believe it's the best option for people so inclined.

I know, however, that direct sales aren't for everyone, and I'm not here to convince you that it's right for you. Rather, I want to share a moment in my life when I was truly knocked down by, yes, direct sales. I was in my early twenties, I'd been doing direct sales for about four months, and I was just about to quit.

Now, I'm not a quitter. I can't even think of a time in my life that I ever quit anything, but at this particular moment, I felt I simply couldn't go any further. I was discouraged: I simply wasn't getting the return on my effort and time that I'd thought I would. I did have a full-time job, so working hard on my direct-sales business in my spare time and getting horrible results was hardly gratifying. I got discouraged every time someone didn't buy. I had become absolutely certain that direct sales wasn't for me. I had no doubt that it was time for me to chalk it up as a lesson learned.

I wouldn't be surprised if my experience resonates with you. I believe most people who enter a direct sales home-based business eventually find themselves in a similar place, and I completely understand why most of those people quit. But, long story short, I got a very timely call from my mentor who, through direct sales, had earned millions of dollars a year for years. This is what he said: "Just remember why you started, and if this job won't help you get what you want out of life, what will take its place? Anything that's worth doing will be harder than you thought. Just take massive action, and the results will come!"

Get Busy!

At first my eyes rolled back in my head. I could only imagine how many people my mentor had said those same words to, but then I realized he was right. I didn't want to be just another person who had tried and failed. I wanted to overcome the odds, not just for the money, but to prove to myself that I could do it. At that moment, in fact, succeeding became more a personal challenge than a business decision, and I took massive action even though I didn't feel like doing so. I literally acted my way into feeling energized to tackle this challenge. And I experienced exactly what Dale Carnegie taught: "Inaction breeds doubt and fear. Action breeds confidence and courage. If you want to conquer fear, don't sit at home thinking about it. Go out and get busy!" And people with a high Grit Factor? They get busy!

So, I got busy! And at the ripe old age of twenty-three, I even became the company's top producer that year. I received a $50,000 bonus check, two tickets to the Super Bowl, and transportation on Jim Carey's private jet! Yes, the famous movie actor's jet!

As we took off, I remembered how close I'd been to giving up. Fear, discouragement, and doubt had me stuck. Immobilized. Hopeless. The cure: massive action! Throughout the rest of my twenties and into my early thirties, I earned millions of dollars more—and of course that would have never happened if I had quit. Today, I own a direct-sales company that allows and empowers thousands of people to truly change their lives. And it's not a business for me; it's a passion.

It Gets Messy!

You may totally relate to the fear, discouragement, and doubt I experienced early in my direct sales days. To keep those very real feelings from robbing you of the desire to reach your true potential, I want to say to you what my mentor said to me: "Inaction breeds doubt and fear. Action breeds confidence and courage. If you want to conquer fear, don't sit at home thinking about it. Go out and get busy!" But simply being busy isn't the solution; what you're busy doing matters.

Judging by the fact that 95 percent of the population is still shuffling their feet at the bottom of Success Mountain, I'd venture to say that whatever all those folks are doing, it's not in alignment with their goals, their dreams, or their bullseyes. Motivational speaker Tony Gaskins says, "If you don't build your dreams, someone will hire you to help build theirs." Steve Jobs said it like this: "Your time is limited, so don't waste it living someone else's life." And people with a high Grit Factor have no trouble acting on this wisdom. These super achievers act readily and unwaveringly in alignment with their bullseyes. To quote Zig Ziglar again: "Outstanding people have one thing in common: an absolute sense of mission." There are no wasted movements. Their energy and time are their most valuable resources. Focused, they take massive action on a consistent basis toward their bullseyes! And let me tell you, it gets messy! Messy? Yes! With massive action comes massive failure!

Many years ago, a young worker asked Tom Watson, then the head of IBM, the key to his success. Watson replied simply, "Double your rate of failure!" Tom Watson knew what every super achiever knows: success and failure are two sides of the *same* coin. You can't have one without the other. Tom Watson knew that success comes when we have twice as many victories as we do losses. I myself learned early on that every failure got me one step closer to a win. The only debilitating failure is ceasing to try. Celebrate the failures knowing that's just practice for celebrating your ultimate success.

Ready... Aim...

The fact is, when all is said and done, usually *more* is *said* than *done*. As we all know, it's easier to talk about what we're going to do than it is to actually do it. It's also easier emotionally to get ready and to aim. So that's what most people do. They get ready... They aim, aim, aim, aim, aim, aim... But they never pull the trigger! Super achievers, however, pull the trigger! They fire, fire, and fire again!

Odds are, many of you reading this book are still aiming—and you'll put this book down only to pick up yet another book. I call that *creative procrastination*. You'll do *anything* to keep from doing what you most need to do, and what you need to do is pull the trigger. Don't stay stuck always aiming but never firing. Yes, reading good books is absolutely vital, but so is taking action. Do both. Avoid paralysis by analysis. In life we typically regret all that we didn't do, not those things we actually attempted.

Do you know why experts tell authors, "Publish your book when it's 80 percent complete?" Why not wait till its 100 percent complete? Because those experts know a book is *never* 100 percent complete! When I published my first book, *Stout Advice*, there were typos. I had people calling me saying, "Logan, did you see that typo on page 27?" Yep, so what! Don't they know that perfection equals paralysis? If I'd waited till my book was *perfect*, it never would have reached the publisher!

So my message to you is… stop waiting. Fear is an ugly monster, and its favorite food is time. In fact, fear grows when you feed it more and more time. If you want to kill fear, as I'm sure you do, then *starve* it of its favorite food. Don't give it any more time. Stop waiting. Take action! Pull. The. Trigger! And you'll be amazed. Like steam rising from a hot cup of coffee, your fear will disappear.

Action Steps to Increase Your Grit Factor:

- Think back to a time you felt fear disappear the moment you took action. What finally compelled you to act? In your current situation what might compel you to act? Why won't you simply act?

- In what aspects of your life can you be more active in your pursuit of your bullseyes? What actions could you take? Choose at least one to do this week.

- In what ways, if any, is your environment encouraging you to take more action? What might you do to make your environment encourage action?

- Are the people you associate with action oriented? Who is the most action-oriented person you know? What will you do to increase the time you spend with this person?

- Having spent some time thinking about how action oriented you are, revisit your six bullseyes. Applying your new understanding and self-awareness, update the Downhill Habits. Then add to or fine-tune the Uphill Habits that will replace the Downhill and enable you to more actively pursue the bullseye in every aspect of your life.

Chapter 20

CONSISTENCY

The secret of success is constancy to purpose.
—Benjamin Disraeli

Webster's defines *consistent* as "unchanging in nature, standard, or effect over time." When applied to a person's behavior and character, this definition reminds me of *authenticity*. You're the same person Friday night as you are Sunday morning. You are consistent in conduct and conversation.

Of all the components of your Grit Factor, I believe that *consistency* is the least talked about and therefore most overlooked. No wonder *consistency* is the factor keeping most people from reaching the top of Success Mountain. Consider, for instance, how consistent your thoughts are. Your mind-set can either help or hurt you; it can be your greatest asset or your greatest liability. If we're *consistently* fearful, discouraged, and full of doubt, we're going to struggle. However, if we're *consistently* fearless, courageous, and confident, success is within reach. After all, most great accomplishments are the result of doing the right things repeatedly, over an extended period of time, with excellence.

Consistency in What Matters Most

I want you to hear a friend's take on what most people are doing with their lives:

> Let's look at the average week for the typical person in America, starting with Saturday night, to see how *consistency* is lacking in most people's lives. On Saturday night, the average person parties hard, stays up late, and fills their body with toxic food and drink, all in the name of having a good time. Sunday morning they sleep in and start the hangover-recovery process. Monday morning, they wake up, still not 100 percent recovered from the weekend, and they reluctantly stumble into work. Tuesday, they're starting to get into a groove. Wednesday and Thursday, they're hitting their stride… but that only lasts until about noon on Friday. On Friday afternoon, they've virtually left the building: they have completely checked out mentally! They go out Friday night. They do a few chores on Saturday. And then they are out on Saturday night. And the cycle has begun again.

I think my friend's take is a bit harsh, but I understand his point. And it is indeed valid.

The sad truth is, most people spend more time planning a vacation than they do planning their life. Ask them to spend a couple hundred dollars to attend a Leadership Summit, and they look at you like you're an idiot. Show them how they can get into the best party in town for

$200, everything included, and you're their hero. As for parents, we (I'm including myself) will do anything and everything for our children, and we too often fail to invest the time necessary to keep our marriages and our personal life growing. We end up spending only our leftover time on ourselves and spouses. No wonder so many marriages end—and some of those that haven't ended simply haven't *officially* ended yet! I'm simply speaking the truth here, and I'm arguing that we must be more consistent in doing the things that matter most.

How consistently do husbands and wives invest time in each other… *without* the kids? How often do couples go on a date night, just the two of them, or perhaps even attend to a leadership conference *together* to invest in their personal growth? You get the point, I hope. Success requires consistency in the little things because those little things add up to the big things. Most people, however, devalue and dismiss the little things. They wrongly think the little things don't matter. Well, a big breakthrough in your life is nothing more than the consistent practice of the little things all adding up. Consistency is key.

Seinfeld's Secret

I want to share with you another important truth that super achievers understand and live: *Successful people do daily what everyone else does occasionally.* That's it. And this truth is worth writing on your mirror, putting on your car visor, or posting on your refrigerator. It is the unsexy secret that no one wants to talk about.

Jerry Seinfeld didn't talk much about this secret; he simply lived it. We know his show, we know his face, we know his name, but few of us know his secret to productivity that fueled his astronomical rise from small-time comic to TV superstar. Early in his career, Seinfeld realized that the way to get ahead in comedy was to have better jokes and that the way to create better jokes was to write *every day*. So he created a system to help him motivate himself.

172 | **GRIT** FACTOR

Seinfeld bought a large calendar and hung it on his wall. His task: *Write jokes for two hours a day.* Once he wrote jokes for two hours, he went to his wall calendar and drew a big red X on the box for that day. And here's what happened:

> After a few days [of drawing a big X on the date] you'll have a chain. Just keep at it, and the chain will grow longer every day. You'll like seeing that chain, especially when you get a few weeks under your belt. Your only job next is to not break the chain. *Do not break the chain!*

Unsexy and simple. Hardly rocket science. But Seinfeld's success speaks to the effectiveness of this approach.

You see, he did what no other comic did: he wrote new jokes *every day.* He went for years and never broke the chain. Other comics would write, but not every day. And how many of these other comics ever made it to the Seinfeld level?

Success leaves clues about how it came to be. Today's clue—courtesy of Jerry Seinfeld—is that *successful people do daily what everyone else does occasionally.*

SOS from a DMO

So what do *you* do daily? What is your DMO (Daily Method of Operation)? Each of us needs a daily method of operation if we're going to operate at our best every day. But have you thought much about your DMO? What are some things you could do daily that would move you closer and closer to the goals you want to achieve? Reminder: Choose things that align with your bullseyes. Jim Rohn calls these the "half-dozen." He says, "There are about a half-dozen things that, when done repeatedly over time, make up about 80 percent of how your life turns out."

By definition, a DMO starts off the same *every* day, and that's true for me no matter where I am in the world. I have a daily devotional emailed to me every morning, and I start my day by reading it. This truth fuels my heart and mind before the world tries to sabotage me. These quiet moments serve as my mental, spiritual, and emotional workout for the day. Next, I work out physically. (We all live in one home our entire lives—and that home is our body! We need to take care of it.) After I shower and before I go into the office, I catch up on emails, texts, messages, and any calendaring I need to do. Attending to these tasks allows me to be fully present when I walk into the door of my office. These elements of my DMO help me stay focused and on track every day.

Your DMO is absolutely critical to reaching your full potential. Our daily routine can hugely influence our life—and the key word is *daily*! Not *weekly* and not *whenever I feel like it*. Daily! I want to make this simple, so hold out your hand and count your fingers: one, two, three, four, five. Now, just as five fingers make up your hand, choose five habits that will make up your day. A DMO is that simple. Fifty tasks are too many. Ten is also too many to track. Five is the number. Even a child can count to five. So your five fingers represent your *Five Daily Habits* that, when done with *consistency* over time, will shape your life in healthy, positive, and, yes, successful ways.

Consistency is the glue that allows self-discipline to flourish, and self-discipline is key to consistency. One cannot have self-discipline and lack consistency—and vice versa. Be consistent. Be self-disciplined. Be the best you possible!

Action Steps to Increase Your Grit Factor:

- What are your *Five Fingers*? List the *Five Daily Habits* that you do or could do.

- Having spent some time thinking about how consistent your behaviors are, revisit your six bullseyes. Applying your new understanding and self-awareness, update the Downhill Habits. Then add to or fine-tune the Uphill Habits that will replace the Downhill and enable you to be more consistent in every aspect of your life.
- Look back at your *Five Fingers*. Be sure they are in alignment with your bullseyes.
- Buy a wall calendar and try Jerry Seinfeld's approach to self-motivation and success. Start your chain and every day decide not to break the chain! Not now! Not ever!

Chapter 21
LOVE

If you would be loved, love, and be lovable.
—Benjamin Franklin

One of the biggest things I see holding people back from reaching their goals is a focus on either the tangible things that success requires or the tangible things that come with success. The reality is, people will never reach their true potential if they don't understand love.

The word *love* is very simple on the surface, but profound in meaning and absolutely essential to living out one's purpose in life. We'll look at four key aspects of the ability to love, to be loved, and to understand the connection between your *love quotient* and your Grit Factor:

1. Love for ourselves
2. Love for others

3. Love for the process
4. Love for the *why*

Love for Ourselves

First and foremost, we must **love ourselves**. *You gotta love you some you!* You are unique and special. God put you on this earth to leave a one-of-a-kind imprint everywhere you go and on everyone you do life with, and it's an imprint only you can leave. God is crazy about you.

And just as God loves you, you must love yourself. I don't mean arrogant, selfish, I'm-better-than-other-people kind of love. Quite the opposite. I mean humble, yet confident secure-in-your-own-skin love for yourself because you love you. To do anything great in life, you have to have unshakable confidence. The foundation of that unshakable confidence is truly loving yourself.

So let me ask you a question: How do you see yourself? Your answer certainly impacts your love for yourself, and your answer can have a significant impact on your life. If, for instance, someone has a low self-image—a low love for self—I can assure you that person is likely afraid most of the time. These individuals see problems, people, positions, and circumstances as *bigger* and *stronger* than they are. Their own self-image leaves them paralyzed and helpless in the face of life's challenges. It also means an inner void that they may try to fill by pleasing other people or trying to get others to like them. Due to this emptiness, they too easily become yes people, and they spend way too much time serving everyone *except* themselves. Consequently, their health, finances, and relationships often suffer.

Because these individuals don't love themselves, they are weak and in desperate need of others to love them. In light of that need, they'll oftentimes not speak their mind for fear of what others will think, or they will be insecure but over-the-top braggadocios. These same people have a hard time making decisions: they may be afraid to offend anyone, or they make decisions based on emotion, past hurts, or a variety of other issues. To these people I say, "Wake up! You gotta love you some you!"

Back to the question "How do you see yourself?" Look at people who have a high self-image—a high love for self. These individuals likely don't care what others think of them. They're not looking to fill some inner empty void with love and approval from other people because there is no void. Confident people genuinely love, appreciate, and respect themselves. They are whole, standing on a firm foundation of love for themselves. No challenge seems too big because they see themselves as *bigger* than the challenge. They hold themselves to high standards, they dress well, they take care of their body, they feed their mind good things daily, and they feed themselves the highest quality foods possible because they see themselves as *deserving*. Bottom line, they know the best investment they will ever make is in themselves.

Speaking of deserving, I think too many people give up on their dreams because they don't think they deserve the happiness that would result. They don't think they're worth the effort or the time. They don't have a deep enough appreciation and love for themselves. The worst thing that happens with this mind-set is that when you *don't* believe in and love yourself, you're sure as heck not going to have a deep love for other people. In order to love other people, the way they deserve to be loved, first, you must love yourself.

Learning to Love Myself

My wife, Haley, and I have known each other since seventh grade, but we didn't date until after high school. I always tell her she would have never dated me back then, and she always replies, "You never asked!"

As a kid, I was the most insecure person I knew. Only when I was in the classroom or playing sports was I secure. Everywhere else I was a disaster. I literally struggled to walk in the hallways of my junior high for fear I'd trip and everyone would see me. I never wanted to say the wrong thing. No wonder I preferred to be by myself. Even then, I had the biggest crush on Haley. Her mom and dad wanted us to date, and my parents always asked me why I didn't ask Haley out. But she had clearly relegated me to the Friend Zone. I'll never forget her calling me for boyfriend advice. I about puked as she blabbed on and on about the dude! He was probably a great guy, but I finally gave her my sage advice: *Break up with him!*

In high school I started to become more secure and confident. I realized I was created in God's image and for a specific purpose. I was God's masterpiece created to do great things.

Now, fast-forward to six years post high school. Haley and I hadn't spoken or seen each other in five years. I was playing pro baseball at the time, but I'd hurt my arm and was on the disabled list. One day, when I had just finished practice, I stopped by my favorite smoothie shop. By this point in my life, on a one-to-ten confidence scale, I was—thank God!—at least a nine.

So I was sitting in a booth sucking down a smoothie and talking baseball with a teammate when in walked Haley and her mother! I couldn't believe it—and, conveniently, I was 100 percent single!

"Haley! How are you? I haven't seen you in forever! Are you married? Kids? Update me!" I said.

Her mother replied before Haley could say a word: "She is single! Totally single!"

Haley, with completely red cheeks, said, "Thanks, Mom!"

Long story short, we went out that night, got engaged four months later, and were married a year after that. When asked how I got upgraded from the Friend Zone to husband, Haley says, "He just grew up. He was always shy and nice, but he just grew up."

What she means is "Now Logan knew who Logan was, and I wanted to be a part of his journey." My looks hadn't changed much, but my self-confidence and love for myself had 100 percent changed. So Haley was suddenly attracted to me. After all, people want to do life with people they can trust. People who know who they are and where they are going. This truth applies in all aspects of life, including business, sales, sports, and relationships. Don't expect people to want to do life with you if you aren't excited to do life with yourself! Love you some you!

Love for Others

The second aspect of love we're going to consider is **love for others**. Understand, this love is *not* a love for people because of what they can *do* for you; this is instead a genuine love for people. And we love them by adding value to their lives. We choose a relational mind-set rather than a transactional mind-set.

And that relational mind-set enables us to achieve great things in life: you are going to bring other people along, and others are going to bring you along. I am certain that everything I've accomplished in my life is a direct result of people helping me along the way. In other words, I've never done anything on my own. I loved and valued other people. At the same time, they loved and valued me, and they spent time with me. They lifted me to heights I could never have reached by myself, and I hope I was able to help them in the same way. Also, if you want people to come along on your journey, they have to believe wholeheartedly that you wholeheartedly believe in them. The foundation of your belief in them is your love for them. They have to know you value the relationship. No one wants to be treated like a number.

Since God made me a people-person, I don't really have trouble loving people. In fact, every time I have the honor of speaking to a team, a company, an organization, or even my own company events, my favorite part is meeting the people who attend. I'll take photos, sign books, and give handshakes and hugs until I get to every person willing to stand in line to meet me. I want them to know that I appreciate them not only because they wanted to meet me, but also because God put each of these one-of-a-kind people on this earth to do great things, to leave this world better than they found it. So I truly consider it an honor to get to meet anyone who wants to say hello.

High Standards, Tough Love

Now being CEO in my own companies gives me countless opportunities to love and serve more people and doing so is both an honor and a responsibility. This mind-set enables me to lead to the best of my ability.

That said, you may have heard that I'm not the easiest guy on the planet to work for—and I promise you that's true. The reason? I demand excellence, and where there is not excellence, I make my disappointment very clear in face-to-face, heart-to-heart, but not usually very peaceful or pleasant conversation. But that is my approach so people have no doubt when I'm upset. In fact, the people I work with know my standards, and they know *where* I'm coming from. They know I'm not speaking *at* them but *with* them because they know *I love them.* They therefore understand that my job is to bring out the best in them for their good and, yes, the company's as well. I fail as a leader if I allow people to be anything less than their best.

I truly believe my success is a result of my deep love and genuine care for people. Loving others has skyrocketed my success journey. In fact, if it weren't for my deep love for other people, I wouldn't be writing this book. The heartbeat behind this book is my desire to help each and every reader know with 100 percent certainty that they can *be, do,* and *have* far more than they currently do. I know for a fact that each and every reader—as well as all the people who aren't reading this book—are capable of achieving so much more than their current lives suggest. Whether I choose to do so through sports, business, one-on-one coaching, or public events, my passion is helping people reach their potential. And that passion is simply a byproduct of my deep love for other people. The greatest leader of all time taught us that the great commandments are to love him and to love others.

Bottom line as I've said, individuals play the game, but teams win championships. The glue that brings the team together and keeps them together is love. And love makes the difference between mere cooperation and heartfelt collaboration. I'll give you a quick example. A group of people working at the same company or wearing the same uniform isn't necessarily a team. They may cooperate with each other, but they may not be entirely on the same page. Those people with a common purpose, goals, and core values, however, are a team. A true team is "all for one and one for all." The people on such a team will have differences, but they will agree to disagree on things—and they will love each other.

Understand, I'm not saying everything is always sunshine and rainbows. Far from it! Even with love, you're going to have your quarrels, and you're going to face arguments that arise because of differences in personality, spirituality, political views, and more. But love is the binding agent that brings together people from all walks of life, all with different views, and then makes that gathering of people one. True teams love each other for who they are as individuals, not just for what they can do for the group.

Choosing to Love the Process

Third, **love the process**. One of things I can't stand to hear is "I have to…" The sentence may end in a variety of ways: "I have to go work out"; "I have to go to the store"; "I have to cook dinner" or "I have to go to a meeting." When I hear people say things like this, I realize their mind-set is off. They are playing the victim. They would be better off—and they would increase their Grit Factor—if they chose to love the process. Of the four loves, I believe that this *loving the process* is the most overlooked and ignored.

Physical fitness is a prime example. We all want to be healthy. That's the desired result, and working out, eating wisely, and getting enough sleep is the *process* that takes us there. Have you ever found yourself thinking, *I have to work out*? Now pause for a moment and consider the millions of people who aren't able to work out. Many of them are too sick or too old. Many of them were born with or have suffered tragic physical limitations, and they can't work out. Considering these people, it seems almost heartless to say, "I have to work out." Actually, that now sounds horrible! Super achievers, however, see the process as a privilege and say with a smile, "I get to work out." Super achievers have an "I get to" mind-set rather than an "I have to" mind-set.

And, of course, my twins offer me a great example of "I get to" vs. "I have to." When they were five years old, they would strategically position themselves on the two toilets farthest away from each other in our house. (I've never witnessed young people game plan against their parents better than Miles and Cooper!) We were blessed in business and our finances are good, so our house was a pretty good size. Picture each of our boys, in opposite wings of the house, both going number two at the same time. And as they magically finished going at the same time, we heard, "Daddy! Mommy! Wipe my butt!" from opposite ends of the house. While that could be annoying— and sometimes it was very annoying—Haley and I realized that the day would come when we'd wish we could hear those two little voices screaming in the distance, "Mommy! Daddy! Wipe my butt!" So even in that situation, we chose to approach wiping butts as we *get* to and not we *have* to. Haley and I were choosing to love the *process* of parenting.

Too many times we get so focused on the end result, in this case, raising a child or two. The truth is, the journey is what makes the end result so rewarding. And the journey is where the memories are made. So, right now, I don't want to think about my kids going off to college. I'm going to miss hearing their voices. I'm going to miss them waking me up in the middle of the night to climb into bed with us. I'm going to miss making them breakfast each morning before they go to school. I'm going to miss all that because I've chosen to embrace and I've learned to love the process of raising my children. Trust me, we parents fall into the victim mind-set plenty of times, just as I have in business, sports, and every other aspect of life. But a high Grit Factor enables us to quickly bounce back into the ownership mind-set. Low Grit Factor means staying stuck in the victim mind-set. Remember, you don't *have to*. You *get to*!

And this choice is just as important in sports even at the highest level. I'll share an example from January 2018. On the eve of his sixth national championship victory, Nick Saban, one of the most successful coaches in the history of college football, was asked what key message he was giving his players hours before the biggest game of their lives. Saban said, "My message to our players is simple: Focus on the process. Focus on the process, and the result will take care of itself. Focus on what you gotta do in each play, in each moment."

What processes do you get to do in your life? I promise you, individuals who embrace and love the process—who have a *get to* mind-set rather than a *have to* mind-set—will have much better results because they have a much better mind-set and a more positive attitude for the journey. The great thing is, no matter who you are or where you are, you can adopt the super achiever's *get to* mind-set right here, right now. Apply this *get to* mind-set in all six areas of life: mental, spiritual, physical, financial, emotional, and relational. Choose to have a *get to* mind-set. You'll be choosing to love the process!

Loving the *Why*

The fourth and final kind of love that grows our Grit Factor is **love of the *why***. We just discussed the love of the process, of the journey, and every process and journey should have a bullseye, a goal you're trying to achieve. Whatever that bullseye is, you must be *in love* with it. If you're involved in business, your bullseye may be to get out of debt, establish a solid retirement for you and your spouse, or build a billion-dollar empire. Whatever your dream, achieving it will take long hours and exhausting days. You'll have to make sacrifices, like missing your kids' games because you're out of town on business or their first recital because you're still at the office working late to secure the future for them.

Let me be clear. It's not that you gotta love the work. Rather, you gotta love the *why* behind that hard work. After all, working hard can be pretty frustrating at times, especially for entrepreneurs and solopreneurs. Maybe your entrepreneurial vision is a second source of income for you, so you have to allocate the time to operate the business. I strongly believe in family first. I do *not* believe you should become a workaholic and miss the most valuable moments of your family's life. You can get money back, but you can't get those moments back. Maintaining a healthy balance is both the goal and the challenge. Sacrifice will be necessary, but don't sacrifice your family along the way. Being a great family man is a lot more important to me than being a billionaire. It's a good thing for all of us that we can do both. We don't have to choose between the two.

And that's an important aspect of the message I share when I'm honored to speak around the world. I truly enjoy adding value to every single person's life whether one-on-one or in a large crowd. When I speak, I often encounter opportunities to remind people to consider their *why*. I ask them, "What strong reason do you have to push just a little bit more, go just a little bit harder, and work just a little bit later?" I ask them: "What is your *why*?" More often than not, our *why* is a *who*.

It's a person, or several people, and usually close family. Our *why* is the group of individuals counting on us to go the distance. Family is often people's *why*. And you know what I'm going to say. Once people identify their strongest *why*, I suggest they put up reminders of it.

My Strongest *Why*

I had an opportunity to dig deep for my strongest *why* on October 11, 2005—eleven days before Haley and I were to be married. I was speaking in front of a packed crowd when I suddenly felt a sharp pain in my abdomen. The pain got sharper and more excruciating every minute. It got so intense that I had to wrap up the speech and immediately get to safe ground—my bed! Thankfully, I was speaking in my hometown; I didn't have to board a plane and fly home.

My infinitely wise fiancée advised me to go to the hospital. I, being the idiot I am, ignored Haley and proceeded to rid my body of every single bit of food and drop of liquid in me—against my will, of course—for twenty-four hours straight. I thought it was really bad food poisoning, but when I couldn't even swallow water, I knew something was seriously wrong. It got so bad I couldn't stand on my own, and I asked Haley to rush me to the emergency room. By this point I was pretty much out of it, but I recall being sent directly into the operating room. Next thing I knew, I was being wheeled out after emergency appendectomy surgery! My appendix had ruptured. I had been literally hours from death and hadn't realized it.

I remember looking up from my hospital bed and seeing Haley, my mom, and the surgeon who saved my life. I remember my mom asking the surgeon how long I'd be in the hospital. The surgeon said no less than fourteen days, but more likely a month or more. At this point I was happy to be alive, but I immediately noticed Haley crying. "What's wrong, baby? I'm alive. No matter how long it takes, at least I'm alive."

My mom said, "Honey, your wedding is in eleven days."

Oh no! I'd completely forgotten about the wedding. A few hours later, when I was alone with the medical team, I told them I was getting married, and we had hundreds of people attending our wedding. I also told them I was *not* going to miss it. No way would I ruin Haley's biggest day, the day she dreamed of as a little girl and had so carefully planned. (Note to all you men out there: Let your bride plan whatever she wants! No charge for this bonus piece of advice.) In this situation I absolutely had my *why*. I was 100 percent in love with Haley and 100 percent committed to making her day perfect. And my showing up was a critical piece of that perfect wedding. I knew I looked horrible after losing a lot of weight in a very short amount of time, but I was determined to be there on October 22, 2005, for our wedding.

I asked the surgeon about the odds of my being able to attend my wedding. I really didn't want to postpone it. Her reply was straightforward—and not what I wanted to hear: "Sir, I'm sorry to tell you this, but there is no way you can make your wedding. I didn't want to tell your bride that, but there's simply no way. People just don't recover fast enough from this type of surgery."

Of course, I had a reply: "Let's say there were a way to leave. What would I have to do for you to let me walk out of here?"

The medical team then gave me a checklist:

1. Pee
2. Poop
3. Drink liquid
4. Drink liquid food
5. Eat real food
6. Stand
7. Walk with aid
8. Walk on my own

There may have been more, but I clearly remember those eight things I knew I had to do in order to walk out of the hospital and marry the woman of my dreams. And this is the part that may freak some of you out, but it's exactly what happened. I had my bullseye: I had the eight things I needed to do in order to hit it. I was all in love with my *why*—with my reason for hitting the mark. Forty-eight hours later I walked out of that hospital on my own!

When the surgeon met with me for the last time, I had one of the most surreal moments of my life. She said, "I've never in my professional career seen anyone walk out of a situation like yours in less than a couple weeks, let alone a couple of days."

I had an explanation: "Well, Doc, thank you for saving my life. I don't know your spiritual views, and in no way would I ever judge them, but I'm a Christian. Although I was fully committed to walking out of here on my own to marry my bride, you told me that was impossible. So, either I'm really good, or God still performs miracles. I'm going to go with the God factor."

She looked at me with a bit of bewilderment and said, "I'm not a Christian, but you certainly piqued my curiosity. There's no way a human being—in his own strength—could accomplish what you did."

I replied, "I agree with you. You gave me the action items, and it looks like God carried me through each one of them."

Regardless of your spiritual views, I assure you my love for my *why*-I-wanted-to-walk-out-of-that- hospital pushed me way beyond my comfort zone. I did things I would never have done without my love for my *why*. Please hear these words: If you don't love the *why* behind what you're doing, the *what* will keep you from succeeding. (You might want to read that sentence again.)

Business, relationships, any aspect of life—can be difficult, frustrating, and discouraging at times. Your *why* is a bulletproof shield that helps you keep going through all the adversity. You show me someone with a strong enough *why*, and I'll show you somebody who can conquer anything.

I believe, though, that too many people are living life without a *why*. They have no bullseye to aim for, so they're just drifting through life rather than intentionally living their life. They aren't designing, much less building, the life of their dreams. They are simply existing. Basically, going through the motions as if life is simply a theme. I so want to tell these folks, there are no do-overs when our time on this earth is done. We have one shot at this. So live intentionally. Establish and aim for bullseyes. Determine the *why* behind everything you're doing. And fall in love with the process of accomplishing your *why*.

Everyone Needs a *Why*

One young man I mentor finally made it into Major League Baseball. During one of our mentoring sessions, I asked him a very simple question: "Now that you're officially a major-league player, what is your *why*?"

I'll never forget his blank expression as he stared back at me. You see, this young man had allowed his entire existence to revolve around his goal of breaking into the majors. As a result, his identity had become being a baseball player. That's not healthy because at some point being a baseball player will end. Then what?

As I've mentioned, most professional athletes go into a deep depression after they retire from the sport that had been their life. I told you earlier about Jonathan Scott, a ten-year NFL veteran. He pointed out that athletes fall in love with being a celebrity and a professional athlete. What a cool identity! But everyone's athletic career ends. And when it does, these "celebrities" are no longer seen or treated as celebrities. People stop asking for their autograph and a selfie with them.

The resulting emptiness can have athletes feeling as if they've lost their entire purpose for living. That's why they need a *why*.

And that's what I wanted the young man I was mentoring to understand. I explained to him exactly what you just read and then asked him again, "What is your *why*?" By the end of the session, he had nailed down his *why*: he wants to add value to people's lives. This *why* became a calling in his life that I have seen him live out day in and day out since then. He uses the platform of baseball to add value to people's lives. That's his *why*. He now evaluates his current career by how many lives he can impact in a positive way, not the statistics or the jersey he's wearing.

Maybe you've experienced—and if not, I truly hope you will experience—what this young man has experienced: he fell in love with his *why*. Now, even in the off-season, he spends most of his time serving those who are less fortunate. I also know for a fact that when his career is over, his *why* will not be. He will transition smoothly into serving people and helping people even more than he does now. In fact, his entire reason for training in the off-season, eating healthy, and getting a good night's sleep every night is to further his ability to invest in his newfound *why*. Without that *why*, he'd just be a baseball player. But because he wants to impact lives and not just run the bases, he has an entirely new energy and motivation for being the very best version of himself he can be.

The Job Is Yours!

I'll never forget the time my wife and I bought a beautiful property with the purpose of building a luxury backyard. My wife handles all this stuff because, quite frankly, I have no desire to. I gave her a very sizable budget so she could build the backyard of her dreams. I did join her as she interviewed the various contractors. At the end of each interview, we'd ask this final question: "What makes you different from all the other companies we're interviewing?" They all had an answer—that I'm sure they regurgitated time after time after time after time. And—don't get me wrong—the answers were all valid and good.

The company we actually hired was represented by a man who gave us a very profound answer to that final question, and his answer was the reason he won the job. He said, "Mr. Stout, I consider it a great honor to build memories for families every time I'm trusted with a project. You and your wife are going to trust somebody to build you memories, not just a backyard. I absolutely love what I do because I love *why* I do it. I can't speak for the other companies trying to earn your business, and I'm certain they would do a great job. What I know for sure is that no one will put their heart and soul into creating the greatest memories possible for your family like I will. This is my passion and my calling in life. On the surface people think I build backyards and swimming pools, but I feel my job is to create memories for those who allow me the honor of working for them."

You're not surprised he got the job, are you? His love for his *why* was great to see.

And that kind of love is only one kind of love that improves your Grit Factor. You gotta love you some you. You have to genuinely love other people. You have to learn to love the process and the journey. And you have to love why you're doing what you're doing. Life isn't always easy. We will always have hardships. But the Grit Factor component that trumps all life throws our way is…love!

Action Steps to Increase Your Grit Factor:

- Do you love *you* some you? If not, why not? What may be keeping you from loving yourself more? What could you do to overcome those obstacles? Also, are you investing in you so you will love you some you?

- Do you love *others*? Offer evidence from your life: where do you act on your love for others rather than just talk about it? What other ways might you live out your love?

- Do you love *the process*? What specific elements keep you fired up? If you aren't loving the process, take time to build a stronger mental and emotional connection between the process and your bullseye.

- Do you have a *why*? If you don't, make it a priority to find one. And if you do, what do you do—and can you do—to fuel your love of that *why*?

- Having spent some time thinking about what and why you love, revisit your six bullseyes. Applying your new understanding and self-awareness, update the Downhill Habits. Then add to or fine-tune the Uphill Habits that will replace the Downhill and enable you to better live out your love in every aspect of your life.

Chapter 22

EPILOGUE: THE HERO'S CALL

You see things; and you say, "Why?" But I dream things that never were; and I say, "Why not?"
—George Bernard Shaw

Y ou may be among the millions who've seen the DC Comics box-office blockbuster *Wonder Woman*. The film opens with a very young Diana, daughter of Queen Hippolyta, aspiring to train and learn to fight like the Amazon warriors who surround her. When her mother finally agrees, the queen tells Diana's teachers to "train her five times and ten times more than any Amazon warrior that has come before her." The queen knows that young Diana will one day have to fight Ares, the god of war. As Diana grows stronger and older, she hears of a raging war led by Ares—a war in which millions of men, women, and children are dying. Feeling a call to help, she says, "I cannot stand by while innocent lives are lost." And the story goes on from there. She answers the call, and Wonder Woman saves the day!

Wonder Woman—like hero stories past and present—follows a pattern. Storytellers refer to it as "the hero's journey." When the story begins, the protagonist—the star of the story—is living in a very ordinary or desolate environment, in an old town or on a small farm. (In *Star Wars,* for example, when we first meet Luke Skywalker, he is living on his uncle's farm.) While at this humble site, the protagonist hears "the hero's call." Luke gets a message from Princess Leah: "Help me! Obi-Wan Kenobi, you are my only hope." Or, in *Wonder Woman,* Diana hears about the war.

In all these stories, however, before the hero is able to answer the call, he or she goes through a transformational process. We watch the hero *develop* into the person who will be able to overcome the mighty challenges they'll inevitably face. So in *Wonder Woman*, Diana trains five and ten times harder than any other Amazon warrior. In *Star Wars*, Luke travels to Dagobah to train with Master Yoda until he is a strong enough Jedi to fight and defeat Darth Vader.

Your Hero Journey

I believe—and clearly Hollywood has demonstrated—that stories of heroes are compelling because, first, each of us relates to the hero on a very deep level and, second, each of us is on a journey of our own. Take a step back and look at your own life. It's not likely you were once living on a planetary farm like Luke, but odds are you aren't living in your dream home now. And I imagine you're probably not working a job that's enabling you to live up to your potential, and studies show that most people don't feel fulfilled at work. It's as if you're Luke Skywalker gazing out at the moon and wanting to be, do, and have more in life! You, too, are hearing a voice inside you saying, *I was meant for more than this!* I believe we all hear this voice, this call to be, do, and have more!

If you've heard that call, what did you do in response? If you're hearing that call now, in what ways are you responding? Your response—whether new or ongoing—may depend on what's going on in your life, and my guess is that you're among the majority of my readers and therefore find yourself in one of three phases of life. The first I call the funk, and in this phase, nothing seems to go right. You find yourself thinking, *can this get any worse? I can't take it!* You may even be crying out those very words to God. But I have good news: We've all been in this kind of funk. In fact, during these times people who don't even believe in God are open to the idea. And during these times we believers start growing again. You see, when everything is going great, it's too easy to lose humility, give ourselves way too much credit for how good life is, and typically stop growing in our faith and in our character. It's the struggles that make us better. So if you're in the funk, know that your setback is setting the stage for an amazing comeback.

Not in the Funk Phase?

The second phase you may be in is the comfortable phase. Things are good. They could be better, but overall, they are comfortable. (This phase is very similar to the Management Mode from the 5 Stages discussed earlier in the book.) But comfort is not our friend! We don't grow when we're comfortable. We become complacent, we put life on cruise control, and we later regret not using our limited days wisely or well. Also, being comfortable is not conducive to reaching your full potential because that only happens when we step out of our comfort zone. Life's great possibilities lie outside our comfort zone. That means that as we aim for our bullseyes, each of us has to become comfortable being uncomfortable.

But here's the bottom line: When my time on earth is done, the last thing I want on my tombstone is *Here lies Logan Stout. Comfortable.* Instead, I want to slide into heaven sweaty and with my knees scraped up and then look God in the eyes and say, "Man, what a ride!" You see, not wanting to be uncomfortable can keep us from doing things, and I think we typically regret the things we *don't* do in life, not the things we actually do. I also have a philosophy: I'm convinced that there's no such thing as a bad experience as long as we learn something from it. The difference between a learning experience and a bad experience is whether or not we grow as a result. So get out of your comfort zone!

A third phase people may be in is freedom. If we're here, we aren't mindlessly drifting through life, and we aren't on cruise control. Instead, we are intentionally designing our life and living according to that design. To be more specific, we are leaving this world better than we found it. We are making a difference for the good in the lives of people around us. And we are passionately chasing our dreams—and not leaving anything on the table. We are going for it! And I'm not talking about going for it only because of making money. Yes, it would be nice to leave an inheritance to the kids, but much more important is leaving a legacy *in* those we love. We are all going to leave a legacy. The only question is, what kind? And as we're soaring freely in this phase, we should wake up excited and go to sleep excited about passionately working toward our bullseyes and living out our *why*. So get out of the funk. Get out of your comfort zone. Be free!

One more thing. You may be concerned because maybe it's been some time since you heard the hero's call for your life. Or maybe life has gotten so busy and noisy that you no longer pay attention to the call ("How could I possibly respond!?!") if you even happen to hear it. Or maybe you thought the call was for someone else. I'm here to tell you, the hero's call is for *you*. And it's *never* too late to respond.

Becoming a Jedi

Before Luke could answer the call and fight Darth Vader, he had to become a Jedi. Like every hero, Skywalker had to experience a transformation. His self-development came as he learned the Jedi skills from Master Yoda, a necessary step before he could face his nemesis.

Notice that the *becoming* precedes the response to the call. Imagine if Luke had immediately gone to fight Darth Vader instead of first training with Master Yoda. The idea is insane! Skywalker wouldn't have had a chance! But that choice to fight first rather than prepare is the exact approach most people take in today's fast-paced society: they want the result *now*! No one wants to put in the legwork first, but that's the only way to set ourselves up for success. There's always something we can be doing *now* to prepare for the role we want. Don't be like unemployed loser Cousin Eddie in *National Lampoon's Christmas Vacation:* "He's holding out for a management position"—and meanwhile doing nothing to improve his leadership skills. That's today's society. Everyone *wants* to succeed, but very few people are working on themselves in order to *become* a person *able* to succeed.

A good example that I've already spoken of is my marriage. As I told you, I had a crush on Haley in high school, but at the time, she had no interest in dating me. But she was the girl I wanted! So how did I get her? I worked, trained, and developed myself, so that years later, when I saw her in the smoothie shop, I had *become* the type of person she found attractive. Preparation breeds confidence and gives us the ability to call up excellence at a moment's notice. In that moment at the smoothie shop, my preparation paid off and, if I do say so, I was pretty excellent. And I had a ring on her finger four months later!

So I'm here to tell you that just as Luke had to become a Jedi and just as I had to grow, you can grow and achieve your dreams. You can hit your bullseyes after you become a Jedi. Your lightsaber—the weapon that will help you overcome your toughest challenges—is a high Grit Factor. Let me give you an all-important question to ask yourself: "What kind of person must I become in order to achieve what I want?" Now I'll give you the answer: a person with a very high Grit Factor!

One more thought. As I travel the world speaking for organizations, teams, and companies, people often tell me that they want my life. When they do, I always ask one simple question: "Are you willing to do what I've done and do to have my life?" The dream is free; the journey costs more than you might think. If you are willing to pay the price, you can live your own dream!

You've heard the hero's call, and you've always wanted to answer that call. But in the back of your mind, you knew that you weren't a Jedi, that you haven't developed the skills you need to successfully answer the call. Perhaps you didn't know what was missing. For 99 percent of people, it's the Grit Factor.

Knowing the *Why*

Let's look at another movie example: *John Wick*. The movie opens with Keanu Reeves's character, John Wick, grieving the recent death of his wife. The movie quickly takes a violent turn when the Russian mob haphazardly steals John Wick's car and kills John Wick's puppy—whom John's dying wife had given him so he'd have company after she was gone. When the puppy dies, John Wick then proceeds to kill dozens of Russian mobsters. His rampage continues throughout the movie until he ultimately takes down the Russian mob... all because they killed his dog.

What I find somewhat humorous about *John Wick* is that we—the audience—see John Wick as the *good* guy in the movie! Crazy! Here is this person going around killing basically anyone with a Russian accent, but because one Russian killed his dog, he's the *good* guy! To the audience, all the killing makes sense because we know the *why*.

I doubt you'll have to confront any Russian mobsters to achieve your dreams, and I certainly pray your puppy doesn't meet a premature and tragic end. However, achieving your dreams *is* going to require getting outside your comfort zone. To achieve what you've never had, you'll have to do things you've never done. Makes sense, doesn't it? Doing those things won't be easy emotionally. Taking these steps will be incredibly hard, and that's why you need a strong *why*. When your *why* is big enough, the *what* you need to do will be easy. And every single human being has a strong *why* if they look for it.

So let me ask you: Why try so hard? Why get up so early? Why push yourself? What is your purpose in life? Why were you born? What is your *why*? Important questions! In fact, Mark Twain said, "The two most important days in your life are the day you were born and the day you find out why." Will today be the day you find out *why*? Maybe you have a vague idea about why you were born. If so, clarify it for yourself. Be as specific as you can. And then amplify it!

As you've read in these pages, I've discovered that the *why* questions of life can often be answered by the *who* questions. So now let me ask you: "Who on the planet do you care about most?" And: "Who out there is counting on you?" Your success isn't simply for your benefit; it's also for those people who are counting on you.

As for my *who*, first and foremost my wife is counting on me. She's counting on me to be a loving husband, a great dad, and a solid family man. She's counting on me to work hard and to provide a financial wall around our family that no one can get through. And that's just the start of the list.

My kids, Miles and Cooper, are also counting on me in a big way. Not a day goes by when I don't ask myself: *Am I being the best dad possible? When I'm home, am I truly present with them? What could I do to better model what it means to be a great husband, dad, leader, coach, person, and follower of God?* If asked these questions at my funeral, what would my family and those closest to me say in response?

And what do you think people might say about you at your funeral?

The Unseen Faces

Vegas billionaire Sheldon Adelson was interviewed on TV about who will inherit his wealth. This comment caught my attention: "I only care about the faces I can see. My unborn grandkids? I don't think about them because they don't exist." Frankly, I don't agree with Mr. Adelson on this. In fact, I believe his kind of thinking to be small. But his quote did get me thinking about the faces I can see as well as the unseen faces in my life.

The faces I can see are those of my wife, my boys, my teammates in business and sports, my friends, my mentors, and the people in the crowds when I speak. I also see the faces of people who show up to meet me, get a picture, or ask for an autograph. And because I can see them, I can impact each one of these individuals today with what I do, with what I say, and by who I am. But I believe I was called to impact more than just the faces I can see.

I am privileged to be able to communicate with countless unseen faces. Like you, the reader of this book, for instance. Also among the unseen faces I might impact are the millions of men and women, boys and girls who will one day read this book or see one of my videos. And thousands will benefit from LoganStout.com offerings and my companies. The unseen faces are also those of my kids' kids' kids! In sum, touching the unseen faces with hope is my legacy!

Your Legacy

Now let's talk about you. Of course the faces you can see are more compelling than the unseen ones. Your dad may be counting on you for financial help after he retires. Your mom has health needs that require your financial support. Other faces you can see are those of your brothers and sisters, your nieces and nephews. It's likely many of these people are your *why*.

Now think about the unseen faces in your life. What impact might you have on your kids' kids' kids? What specifically do you want your legacy to be? As you think about these big questions, imagine the person you will become.... Imagine the people you will impact.... And imagine the lives you will change.

By considering the faces you can see as well as those you can't, your *why* becomes so much bigger than just you. Your *why* also becomes so strong that no obstacle will stand a chance. You'll also quickly and eagerly begin to grow your Grit Factor. In fact, in a matter of time, you'll be doing more than you ever thought possible. You'll be achieving more because you will have become more. And—my prayer and wish for you—may you truly become all that you can be! Your Grit Factor will help that happen.

I am honored that you chose to read this book. I'd be further honored if you would share this book with someone you care about—or if you told the world about it! Also, please connect with me on social media. Let me know your favorite quotes, attributes, lines, and lessons and/or how the book inspired some positivity in your life. Finally, I didn't write this book for me. I wrote it for you and for all who are counting on you, and I hope to meet you soon at one of our events. I love you and pray God's blessings over your life!

ABOUT THE AUTHOR

Logan Stout is an accomplished business owner having generated billions of dollars of revenue throughout his career. He is a philanthropist, entrepreneur, best-selling author, keynote speaker and leadership trainer who makes regular television and podcast appearances and travels the world to educate, motivate and inspire. Logan is passionate about helping individuals, teams and organizations reach their full potential. His first book, Stout Advice: The Secrets to Building Yourself, People, and Teams, empowers and inspires personal growth in readers and aids in reaching God-given potential. Logan shares weekly on his media outlets. He hosts training calls which teach individuals, teams and corporations how to implement strategies to maximize their personal success and development, and add to their business. He has been a featured guest on the majority of television and media outlets in America.

Logan is also the founder and CEO of the Dallas Patriots baseball organization and Premier Baseball Academy in Frisco, Texas, which focus on mentoring and leading youth. This organization is one of the largest in the world, providing select teams ages six through eighteen years old with world-class instructors, coaches, and training. Every graduate of the Dallas Patriots baseball organization has earned the opportunity to play college baseball.

Logan Stout and his wife, Haley, have two sons and reside in Frisco, Texas. They are patrons and honorary chairs of the Boys and Girls Club of Collin County, the American Heart Association of North Texas, founders of Youth

Athletes Foundation and other charitable organizations. Logan holds degrees in both business and psychology.

For inquiries and to book Logan, email info@LoganStout.com.

CPSIA information can be obtained
at www.ICGtesting.com
Printed in the USA
BVHW070053120821
614267BV00001B/79

9 781642 799477